Scientific Computing with Scala

Learn to solve scientific computing problems using Scala and its numerical computing, data processing, concurrency, and plotting libraries

Vytautas Jančauskas

[PACKT] open source✲
PUBLISHING   community experience distilled

BIRMINGHAM - MUMBAI

Scientific Computing with Scala

First published: April 2016

Production reference: 1220416

Published by Packt Publishing Ltd.
Livery Place
35 Livery Street
Birmingham B3 2PB, UK.

ISBN 978-1-78588-694-2

www.packtpub.com

Credits

Author
Vytautas Jančauskas

Reviewer
Chetan Khatri

Commissioning Editor
Amarabha Banerjee

Acquisition Editors
Ruchita Bhansali

Sonali Vernekar

Content DevelopmentEditor
Kajal Thapar

Technical Editor
Prajakta Mhatre

Copy Editor
Charlotte Carneiro

Project Coordinator
Shweta H Birwatkar

Proofreader
Safis Editing

Indexer
Rekha Nair

Graphics
Kirk D'Penha

Production Coordinator
Manu Joseph

Cover Work
Manu Joseph

About the Author

Vytautas Jančauskas is a computer science PhD student and lecturer at Vilnius University. At the time of writing, he was about to get a PhD in computer science. The thesis concerns multiobjective optimization using nature-inspired optimization methods. Throughout the years, he has worked on a number of open source projects that have to do with scientific computing. These include Octave, pandas, and others. Currently, he is working with numerical codes with astrophysical applications.

He has experience writing code to be run on supercomputers, optimizing code for performance, and interfacing C code to higher-level languages. He has been teaching computer networks, operating systems design, C programming, and computer architecture to computer science and software engineering undergraduates at Vilnius University for 4 years now.

His primary research interests include optimization, numerical algorithms, programming language design, and software engineering. Vytautas has significant experience with various different programming languages. He has written simple programs and has participated in projects using Scheme, Common Lisp, Python, C/C++, and Scala. He has experience working as a Unix systems administrator. He also has significant experience working with numerical computing platforms such as NumPy/MATLAB and data analysis frameworks such pandas and R.

I would like to thank my wife for being patient and giving me time to write this book.

About the Reviewer

Chetan Khatri is data science researcher with over four and a half years of experience in research and development. He works as a principal engineer in data and machine learning at Nazara Technologies Pvt. Ltd. Previously, he worked with R&D Lab, Eccella Corporation. He completed his masters in computer science and minor in data science from KSKV Kachchh University and was a gold medalist.

He contributes to society in various ways, including giving talks to sophomore students at University. He also gives talks on various fields of data science at academia and conferences. He helps the community by providing a data science platform, and loves to participate in data science hackathons. He is one of the founding member of PyKutch—a Python community. Currently, he is exploring deep neural networks and reinforcement learning for government data.

I would like to thank Prof. Devji Chhanga, Head of the Computer Science department, University of Kachchh, for showing me the correct path and for valuable guidance in the field of data science research.

I would like to thank my beloved family.

www.PacktPub.com

eBooks, discount offers, and more

Did you know that Packt offers eBook versions of every book published, with PDF and ePub files available? You can upgrade to the eBook version at www.PacktPub.com and as a print book customer, you are entitled to a discount on the eBook copy. Get in touch with us at customercare@packtpub.com for more details.

At www.PacktPub.com, you can also read a collection of free technical articles, sign up for a range of free newsletters and receive exclusive discounts and offers on Packt books and eBooks.

https://www2.packtpub.com/books/subscription/packtlib

Do you need instant solutions to your IT questions? PacktLib is Packt's online digital book library. Here, you can search, access, and readPackt's entire library of books.

Why subscribe?

- Fully searchable across every book published by Packt
- Copy and paste, print, and bookmark content
- On demand and accessible via a web browser

Table of Contents

Preface

In this book, we will look into using Scala as a scientific computing platform. It is intended for people who already have experience with scientific computing and Scala. We will see how to do things that are possible in other numerical/scientific computing platforms in Scala. We will cover numerical computation, data storage and retrieval, structured data analysis, interactive computing, visualization, and other important topics.

What this book covers

Chapter 1, *Introducing Scientific Computing with Scala*, looks into the feasibility of using Scala for scientific computing. An overview of the state-of-the-art libraries and tools in Scala scientific computing is given here.

Chapter 2, *Storing and Retrieving Data*, provides various options for storing and retrieving data in Scala. Popular data storage and retrieval formats that you may encounter in scientific computing are explored.

Chapter 3, *Numerical Computing with Breeze*, is about using the Breeze library for numerical computing.

Chapter 4, *Using Saddle for Data Analysis*, explores the functionality of the Saddle library for structured data analysis and manipulation.

Chapter 5, *Interactive Computing with ScalaLab*, explores the possibilities offered by the ScalaLab environment for interactive computing.

Chapter 6, *Parallel Programming in Scala*, is about parallel programming in Scala. Various techniques, including JVM threads, parallel collections, and actor-based concurrency with Akka, are covered.

Chapter 7, Cluster Computing Using Scala, teaches how to use Scala programs in distributed computing environments and shows how to use MPI from Scala, and more.

Chapter 8, Scientific Plotting with Scala, gives various options for carrying out plots in Scala.

Chapter 9, Visualizing Multi-Dimensional Data in Scala, elaborates on advanced plotting and visualization.

What you need for this book

You will need Scala and SBT installed on your system. Technically, you only need SBT, since SBT will install the required version of Scala for you. You can get Scala and SBT from the following websites:

- http://www.scala-lang.org/
- http://www.scala-sbt.org/

It is advisable that you use a UNIX-like operating system for this book. However, this is not strictly necessary for most chapters. You will also need a Scala IDE or a text editor. Setting up Emacs to work with Scala and SBT is covered in the book. Alternatively, you can use any editor you are comfortable with.

Who this book is for

This book is for scientists and engineers who would like to use Scala for their scientific and numerical computing needs. Basic familiarity with undergraduate-level mathematics and statistics is expected but not strictly required. Basic knowledge of Scala is required as well as the ability to write simple Scala programs. Complicated programming concepts are not used in the book. Anyone who wants to explore using Scala for writing scientific or engineering software will benefit from the book.

Conventions

In this book, you will find a number of text styles that distinguish between different kinds of information. Here are some examples of these styles and an explanation of their meaning.

Code words in text, database table names, folder names, filenames, file extensions, pathnames, dummy URLs, user input, and Twitter handles are shown as follows: "For now, simply create a new folder called `csvreader` and a file in it called `CSVReader.scala`."

A block of code is set as follows:

```
object CSVReader {
    def main(args: Array[String]) {
        for (line <- Source.fromFile("iris.csv").getLines()) {
            println(line)
        }
    }
}
```

Any command-line input or output is written as follows:

```
scala> xs dot ws
res2: Double = 27.5
```

New terms and **important words** are shown in bold. Words that you see on the screen, for example, in menus or dialog boxes, appear in the text like this: "You can access it via the **Plot** menu option."

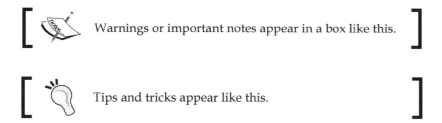

Warnings or important notes appear in a box like this.

Tips and tricks appear like this.

Reader feedback

Feedback from our readers is always welcome. Let us know what you think about this book—what you liked or disliked. Reader feedback is important for us as it helps us develop titles that you will really get the most out of.

To send us general feedback, simply e-mail feedback@packtpub.com, and mention the book's title in the subject of your message.

If there is a topic that you have expertise in and you are interested in either writing or contributing to a book, see our author guide at www.packtpub.com/authors.

Customer support

Now that you are the proud owner of a Packt book, we have a number of things to help you to get the most from your purchase.

Downloading the example code

You can download the example code files for this book from your account at `http://www.packtpub.com`. If you purchased this book elsewhere, you can visit `http://www.packtpub.com/support` and register to have the files e-mailed directly to you.

You can download the code files by following these steps:

1. Log in or register to our website using your e-mail address and password.
2. Hover the mouse pointer on the **SUPPORT** tab at the top.
3. Click on **Code Downloads & Errata**.
4. Enter the name of the book in the **Search** box.
5. Select the book for which you're looking to download the code files.
6. Choose from the drop-down menu where you purchased this book from.
7. Click on **Code Download**.

You can also download the code files by clicking on the **Code Files** button on the book's webpage at the Packt Publishing website. This page can be accessed by entering the book's name in the **Search** box. Please note that you need to be logged in to your Packt account.

Once the file is downloaded, please make sure that you unzip or extract the folder using the latest version of:

- WinRAR / 7-Zip for Windows
- Zipeg / iZip / UnRarX for Mac
- 7-Zip / PeaZip for Linux

Downloading the color images of this book

We also provide you with a PDF file that has color images of the screenshots/diagrams used in this book. The color images will help you better understand the changes in the output. You can download this file from `https://www.packtpub.com/sites/default/files/downloads/ScientificComputingwithScala_ColorImages.pdf`.

Errata

Although we have taken every care to ensure the accuracy of our content, mistakes do happen. If you find a mistake in one of our books—maybe a mistake in the text or the code—we would be grateful if you could report this to us. By doing so, you can save other readers from frustration and help us improve subsequent versions of this book. If you find any errata, please report them by visiting http://www.packtpub.com/submit-errata, selecting your book, clicking on the **Errata Submission Form** link, and entering the details of your errata. Once your errata are verified, your submission will be accepted and the errata will be uploaded to our website or added to any list of existing errata under the Errata section of that title.

To view the previously submitted errata, go to https://www.packtpub.com/books/content/support and enter the name of the book in the search field. The required information will appear under the **Errata** section.

Piracy

Piracy of copyrighted material on the Internet is an ongoing problem across all media. At Packt, we take the protection of our copyright and licenses very seriously. If you come across any illegal copies of our works in any form on the Internet, please provide us with the location address or website name immediately so that we can pursue a remedy.

Please contact us at copyright@packtpub.com with a link to the suspected pirated material.

We appreciate your help in protecting our authors and our ability to bring you valuable content.

Questions

If you have a problem with any aspect of this book, you can contact us at questions@packtpub.com, and we will do our best to address the problem.

1
Introducing Scientific Computing with Scala

Scala was first publicly released in 2004 by Martin Odersky, then working at École Polytechnique Fédérale de Lausanne in Switzerland. Odersky took part in designing the current generation of the Java compiler **javac** as well. Scala programs, when compiled, run on the **Java Virtual Machine (JVM)**. Scala is the most popular of all the JVM languages (except for Java.) Like Java, Scala is statically typed. From the perspective of a programmer, this means that variable types will have to be declared (unless they can be inferred by the compiler) and they cannot change during the execution of the program. This is in contrast to dynamic languages, such as Python, where you don't have to specify a variable's type and can assign anything to any variable at runtime. Unlike Java, Scala has strong support for functional programming. Scala draws inspiration from languages such as Haskell, Erlang, and others in this regard.

In this chapter, we will talk about why you would want to use Scala as your primary scientific computing environment. We will consider the advantages it has over other popular programming languages that are used in the scientific computing context. We will then go over Scala packages meant specifically for scientific computing. These will be considered briefly and will be divided into categories depending on what they are used for. Some of these we will consider in detail in later chapters.

Finally, we provide a small introduction on best practices for how to structure, build, test, and distribute your Scala software. This is important even to people who know how to program in Scala already. This chapter introduces concepts that I consider essential, to write scientific software successfully. They are, however, often overlooked by scientists. The reason is that scientists often don't concern themselves with software development techniques; instead, they prefer to get the job done quickly. For example, it is not uncommon to neglect build systems, which are very important no matter what language you are using and are essential when writing software in statically typed, compiled languages. Testing is another area of software development criminally overlooked by the scientists I have had the pleasure to work with. The same is usually true of IDE's, debuggers, and profilers. All of these following topics will be discussed:

- Why Scala for scientific computing?
- Numerical computing packages for Scala
- Data analysis packages for Scala
- Other scientific software
- Alternatives for carrying out plotting
- Using Emacs as the Scala IDE
- Profiling Scala code
- Debugging Scala code
- Building, testing, and distributing your Scala software
- Mixing Java and Scala code

Why Scala for scientific computing?

This book assumes a basic familiarity with the Scala language. If you do not know Scala but are interested in writing your scientific code in it, you should consider getting a companion book that teaches the basics of the language. Any nontrivial topics will be explained, but we do not provide an introduction to any of the basic Scala programming concepts here. We will assume that you have Scala installed and you have your favorite IDE, or at least your favorite text editor setup to write Scala programs. If not, we introduce using Emacs as a Scala IDE. It would also be of benefit to you if you are already familiar with other popular scientific computing systems.

A lot of the topics in the book will be far easier to understand and put to good use if you already know how to do the things in question in other systems: we will be covering functionality that is similar to the MATLAB interactive computing environment, NumPy scientific computing package for the Python programming language, pandas data analysis library for Python, statistical computing language R, and similar software. After reading the book, you will hopefully be able to get all the functionality of the aforementioned software from Scala and more!

What are the advantages compared to C/C++/Java?

One obvious advantage to using Scala is that it is a Java virtual machine language. It is one among several, including Clojure, Groovy, Jython, JRuby, and of course Java itself. This means that, after writing your program, you compile it to a Java virtual machine bytecode that is then executed by the Java virtual machine interpreter. Think of the bytecode as the machine code of a virtual computer. When you write programs in C/C++ and similar compiled languages, they are translated straight to machine code that you then execute directly on your computer's processor. If you want to then run it on a different processor, you would have to recompile your program. Since the Java virtual machine runs on many different computer architectures, this is no longer necessary.

After you compile your program, the resulting bytecode can then be run on any system that can run a Java virtual machine. Therefore, your compiled code is portable. This is one advantage to using Scala as opposed to C/C++. Why not just write your program in Java then? Java is designed for writing large software in teams consisting of many programmers of varying skill levels. As such, it is an incredibly bureaucratic language. Quickly realizing your ideas in Java is difficult. This is because, even in the simplest cases, there is a lot of boilerplate code involved. The language is designed to slow you down and force you to do things by the book, designing the software before you start writing it.

Scala has the additional advantage of interactivity. It is easy to write and run small Scala programs, test them interactively, make changes, and then repeat. This is essential for scientific code, where a lot of the time you are testing an idea out and you want to do it quickly so that, if it does not work out, you can move on to another idea. As an added bonus, you can use any of the many Java libraries from Scala with ease! Since Java is very widely used in the industry, it contains a plethora of libraries for various purposes. These can be accessed from any JVM-based language. Most often, new functional programming languages don't share this advantage (since they are not JVM-based).

Scala also has strong support for functional programming. Functional programming treats programming as the evaluation of mathematical functions and avoids changing variable state explicitly. This leads to a declarative programming style where (ideally) the intention, rather than an explicit procedure, is given by the programmer. This (partially) eliminates the need for side effects—changes in the program state. Eliminating side effects leads to a programming style that is less error-prone and makes it easier to understand and predict program behavior. This has important consequences such as the easy and automatic parallelization of programs, program verification, and so on.

Parallelization is becoming more important with the increasing number of CPU cores in computers. Parallel programming in imperative languages involves a lot of very subtle issues that few programmers fully understand. So, there is hope that functional programming can help in this regard.

Pure functional programming often feels restrictive to programmers who are used to the more common imperative style. As a consequence of this, Scala supports both programming styles. You can start programming more or less as you would in Java and slowly incorporate more advanced features of the language into your programs. This removes a lot of the seemingly intimidating nature of functional programming since the concepts can be incorporated when needed and where they fit best. This may annoy functional programming purists, but is great for the more pragmatically minded.

Here is a small code segment that compares Java and Scala code, which takes an array, squares the elements, and adds them together. This is not an uncommon pattern (in one form or another) in numerical code. This will serve as a small example of Scala's conciseness compared to Java. This is by no means a proof of how Scala is more concise compared to Java, but the perception that it is is very often true.

Scala code:

```
val arr = (0 until 10).toArray
arr.map(x => x * x).reduce(_+_)
```

Java code:

```
int arr[] = {0, 1, 2, 3, 4, 5, 6, 7, 8, 9};
int result = 0;
for (int a: arr) {
  result += a * a;
}
```

In the Scala version, we think descriptively in functions that are applied to the array to get the result we want. These functions take other functions as arguments. In the Java version, we think imperatively — what actions have to be taken to get the result we need?

What are the advantages compared to MATLAB/Python/R?

You may object that a lot of what has been said earlier can also be said of languages such as Python, MATLAB, R, or any other interpreted language. They all support different programming styles; when you write your program in, say Python, it will run on any platform that can run a Python interpreter. So, why not just use those? Well, one answer is execution speed. Many will object, and have objected before, that speed is not their primary concern when writing scientific software. That is true but only up to a point. It isn't easy to convince people of this, but I have grown convinced of this myself. The usual workflow in languages using dynamic typing is outlined here:

- Prototype your numerically intensive code in your favorite language.
- Note that it will take 3 years to complete a single run of the program in its current state.
- Use a profiler to identify bottlenecks. The profiler indicates that everything is a bottleneck.
- Rewrite the most performance critical parts in C or C++.
- Battle the foreign function interface or whatever other method your language provides for calling C/C++ functions.
- End up with a C/C++ program wrapped in a couple of lines of your favorite programming language.

The aforementioned is obviously a caricature. However, the important point is that the process described here adds at least two extra nontrivial stages to the already complicated process of writing software; not any software, but software you usually have no clear specifications for. On top of that, you are often not sure if what you are doing is sensible (which is the case for most scientific software in my experience).

The two extra stages are using the profiler, which is a tool that identifies portions of the code your program spends time in, and embedding code written in C/C++ (or some other statically typed language) in your program. People often will use a profiler on programs written in languages such as C++ or Java as well. But the reason for using it is usually that you want to squeeze the last few drops of performance out of it and not just make the software usable. The result of this is that all of the advantages of your nice dynamically typed programming language are reduced to nothing.

These advantages are supposed to be the speed of development and being able to make changes quickly. However, you end up spending time profiling software, rewriting nice bits of your code into ugly efficient bits, and finally just writing most of the thing in C. None of this sounds or is fun. There are workarounds to this, but why would you be content with this procedure? Why can't you just write your program and have it behave sensibly from the very start? Some will object that you should not be using a programming language such as Python for performance-critical code. This is true. However, most people learn one language, get used to its libraries, and will tend to write all their code in it.

You may very well end up with something that is not usable without a lot of extra effort this way. Using languages designed for the speed of execution (so called systems programming languages) is certainly possible. They, however, have many other disadvantages. The primary disadvantage is that prototyping is very hard in them. So is realizing your ideas quickly.

So, how does Scala help? Why is it faster than, say, Python; and by how much? Where does dynamic versus static typing come in to this? A simple way to see how much faster one language is when compared to another is to use some kind of benchmark suite. An interesting comparison is provided in the following website:

```
http://benchmarksgame.alioth.debian.org/
```

You can visit the website to make sure what is said here is true. In it, several different algorithms implemented in each different language are compared in terms of execution speed, memory use, and so on. Java is evaluated against C in the results. It can be seen that Java is comparable to C in terms of execution speed. Even though it is slower, it is usually not slower by much. In two cases out of eleven, it is actually faster. The comparisons that are more interesting are between Python 3 and Java, and Scala and Java.

Python is a very popular language in scientific computing. So, how does it stack up? In five cases out of eleven, it is actually around 40 times slower than Java. This is a lot. If your calculations take 10 minutes with Java, you would have to wait almost 7 hours, if you wrote them in Python (if we assume a linear relationship — a fair assumption in this case I feel). Scala is much better in this regard.

In most cases, its speed is compared to that of Java. This is good news, since Java is a fairly fast language. This means that you can write your code in the clearest way possible, and it will still work fast. If you want to squeeze some extra juice out of it, you can always profile it using one of the profiling tools we will discuss later. Would the same apply in the case of MATLAB and R? Well, the website does not benchmark those languages but one would imagine so. Those are both dynamic languages as well.

So what is a dynamic language and a static language? Why is one slower than the other? What other advantages or disadvantages are there in using one over the other? The simplest way to describe it is this: in a dynamically typed language, variables are bound to objects only, and in a statically typed language variables are bound to both object and type.

When you program in a dynamically typed language, you can usually assign anything you want to any variable. In a statically typed language, a variable's type is declared in advance (or in the case of Scala can be inferred from context).

In practice, it follows from this that the compiler can optimize the code much better, since it can use optimizations specific for that type. For example, this happens with Java's numeric types, where they are compiled to JVM arithmetic opcodes instead of more general method calls. In a dynamic language, the type often has to be determined at runtime and there are often other checks as well. All of this consumes CPU cycles.

Furthermore, calling functions and methods as well as accessing object attributes is much faster in static languages than in dynamic ones. A compiler is also capable of catching type errors. In a dynamic language such as Python, nothing prevents you from calling any method with any arguments on any object. This leads to problems since these errors are only caught at runtime.

It can easily happen that your program will fail near the end of a 2-hour run just because you forgot that you made changes to a method's argument list. In statically typed languages, these types of error will be caught at compile time. As an added bonus, good IDEs are easier to implement for static languages than for dynamic ones. This is because the code itself provides a lot of useful information that the IDE can use to provide functionality you expect from a modern IDE. This includes autocompletion, listing available methods for an object, and so on.

Let's recap what was said so far — the main advantage to using Scala for scientific code is that you can write what you mean, and it will usually work fast. There is no need for elaborate and often wonky strategies employed to optimize code in other languages. This will result in readable, easy-to-understand code, and you will not lose any of the advantages of dynamic languages.

Scala is quick to develop in and easy to understand. I think these are the main reasons why you should consider it as your main scientific computing language. This is especially true if you write your own numerical code or code that is generally fairly complex and where you can't rely on fast libraries to provide most of the functionality.

Scala does parallelism well

Parallel execution of code is very important in scientific computing. Often scientists want to model a certain physical phenomenon. Simulations of the physical world take a long time. Since the primary method of increasing computer performance is adding more CPU cores, parallelizing your algorithms is becoming the main way of reducing the amount of time it takes your program to do the things you want of it.

Another aspect of this is running code on supercomputers where algorithms are split up into several tasks that usually communicate by passing messages to each other. Programs written in imperative style are generally tricky to parallelize. Scala has strong support for functional programming. In general, the declarative nature of programs written in functional programming languages makes them easier to parallelize. The main reason for this is that functional programming languages avoid side effects.

Side effects are explicit changes to state, such as assigning to variables, writing to files, or devices. Avoiding side effects avoids common pitfalls in parallel programming such as, race conditions, deadlocks, and so on. While no technique avoids these problems completely, declarative programming languages are much better suited to handle these issues.

Scala supports parallel collections that make it easy to carry out concurrent calculations. Another option is to use the Akka toolkit that supports several ways of carrying out calculations in parallel. Both these options will be discussed in detail in the following chapters.

Any downsides?

There is currently one big downside to using Scala for scientific computing, and many would consider it a crucial one; there currently aren't many well-established packages for scientific computing available for it. While the core language is solid, without an established infrastructure of libraries, there is only so much you can do on your own.

The situation in this regard is a lot better in other systems. This is especially true of Python, which has more scientific computing libraries than you can shake a stick at. But, it is also true of MATLAB and others. Thus, is the nature of the vicious cycle of popularity—systems are popular because they have many libraries for doing different things, and they have many libraries because they are popular.

Scala isn't yet an established language in this regard. I believe, however, that it deserves to be. And, maybe this book will help it towards that goal. With enough people using Scala for scientific computing, we will eventually see more libraries developed and existing ones being better supported and more actively maintained.

Numerical computing packages for Scala

Let's now look through linear algebra and numerical computing software that is available for Scala. A linear algebra software package would involve being able to perform operations on matrices and vectors, solving linear systems of equations, finding the determinant, and performing other operations associated with the discipline of linear algebra in the field of mathematics.

MATLAB started as a linear algebra package and evolved into a whole programming language and interactive computing environment. The NumPy library for Python can do most of the things expected from a linear algebra package and a lot more. In this section, we will provide an overview of what is available in Scala in this regard. We will examine the packages briefly, tell you where to get them, how actively they are developed, and very briefly discuss the main functionality available in them.

Scalala

Scalala is a linear algebra package for Scala. It is currently not actively maintained, having been superseded by Breeze. It can be found at the following website:

```
https://github.com/scalala/Scalala
```

It is right now mostly of historic interest; however, Scalala has rich MATLAB-like operators on vectors and matrices and a library of numerical routines. It also has basic support for plotting.

Breeze

Breeze is the biggest and best maintained numerical computing library for Scala. It can be found at the ScalaNLP website:

http://www.scalanlp.org/

It is developed along with Epic and Puck, the former of which is a powerful statistical parser and the latter is a GPU-powered parser for natural languages. These two later libraries will be of less concern to us. Breeze, however, is a big part of this book. It provide functionality that is roughly equivalent to the famous and widely used NumPy package for Python. It is actively maintained and is likely to remain so in the near future.

Breeze is modeled on Scalala, which was mentioned previously. It supports all the matrix and vector operations you would expect. It provides a large number of probability distributions. It also provides routines for optimization and linear equation solving as well as routines for plotting. In a later chapter, we will introduce Breeze in detail and explain to readers how to do things they have grown accustomed to in other systems in Breeze.

ScalaLab

ScalaLab is a numerical computing environment aiming to replicate the functionality of MATLAB. The website is given here:

https://code.google.com/p/scalalab/

ScalaLab will be discussed in a section dedicated to it. It supports Scala-based scripting and is written mostly in Java with some speed-critical sections written in C/C++. It allows you to access the results of MATLAB scripts. It can use dozens of Scala and Java libraries for scientific computing. There is a basic support for plotting:

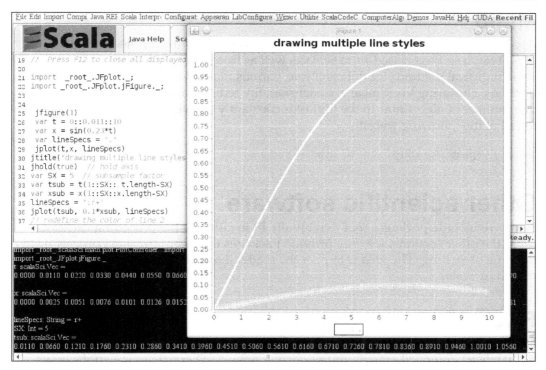

The ScalaLab window with a plotting example

Data analysis packages for Scala

By data analysis packages, we mean software designed for analyzing data in some way. A simple statistical regression would be an example. Software implementing machine-learning algorithms would be another example.

Saddle

Saddle is Scala's answer to R and Python's pandas package. It supports reading in structured data in a variety of different formats, including CSV and HDF5. The data can be loaded into frames and then manipulated as you would in other similar software. Statistical analysis can be performed, and you can build your own statistical analysis methods on top of the data structures provided by Saddle. Saddle is examined in detail in a separate chapter dedicated to it. It can be found at the following website:

```
https://saddle.github.io/
```

MLlib

Apache's MLlib library provides machine learning algorithms for the Spark platform. The library can be accessed from Scala as well as from Java and Python. It supports basic statistical methods for data analysis, various regression and classification methods, clustering via k-means, dimensionality reduction, and optimization methods. The number of algorithms in the library is constantly growing. The MLib library can be found at the following website:

```
http://spark.apache.org/mllib/
```

Other scientific software

Here, we include packages that don't really fit in either of the preceding categories. As in the other sections, we only provide packages that seem the most promising at the time of writing. The idea is to give the reader a sense of what's available in this regard in Scala.

FACTORIE

FACTORIE is a toolkit for deployable probabilistic modeling. It allows you to create probabilistic graphical models and perform inference. There are many applications for probabilistic graphical modeling including speech recognition, computer vision, natural language processing, and applications in bioinformatics. For more information on FACTORIE, refer to the following website

```
http://factorie.cs.umass.edu/
```

Cassovary

Cassovary is a large graph processing toolkit developed by Twitter. While there are other graph libraries for Scala, Cassovary allows one to work with graphs consisting of billions of vertices and edges in an efficient way. It powers the underlying Twitter infrastructure. Here is the link for Cassovary:

```
https://github.com/twitter/cassovary
```

Figaro

Figaro is a probabilistic programming language. It supports the development of rich probabilistic models and provides reasoning algorithms. These can be used to draw conclusions from evidence. Probabilistic reasoning is one of the foundational technologies behind machine learning. It has been used for stock price prediction, recommendation systems, image detection, and other machine learning tasks. For more information on Figaro, visit:

```
https://github.com/p2t2/figaro
```

Alternatives for doing plotting

There are many ways of doing plotting in Scala. We will discuss most of these in the chapters dedicated to plotting. For the time being, we will give a small summary. Breeze, Saddle, and ScalaLab all have basic support for plotting. Wisp stands out as a library worth mentioning:

```
https://github.com/quantifind/wisp
```

You can use Jzy3d for 3D plots:

```
http://jzy3d.org/
```

You can also use Java libraries for plotting. Among these, JFreeChart can be considered as being a roughly equivalent feature to libraries such as matplotlib:

```
http://www.jfree.org/jfreechart/
```

Using Emacs as the Scala IDE

If you haven't yet picked a Scala IDE to use, I would like to recommend the ENSIME mode for Emacs and other editors. You can find it at the following website:

```
https://github.com/ensime
```

Obviously installation instruction will be dependent on the kind of editor you are using. If using it with Emacs (a popular cross-platform editor), the installation process is described here. You can get Emacs from the Emacs website:

```
https://www.gnu.org/software/emacs/
```

There are a lot of books available on using it. It is completely open source and with ENSIME it makes probably the best open source IDE for Scala, in the author's opinion. After installing Emacs on your system, you can install ENSIME. To do this, first add the following lines to your `.emacs` file, which (on Linux) usually resides in your home directory. If you are not using Linux, consult the Emacs documentation for where the `.emacs` file is. The following code assumes a fairly recent version of Emacs. This was tested with Emacs 24:

```
(require 'package)
(add-to-list 'package-archives
             '("melpa" . "https://melpa.org/packages/"))
(when (< emacs-major-version 24)
  (add-to-list 'package-archives '("gnu" . "http://elpa.gnu.org/
packages/")))
(package-initialize)
(require 'ensime)
(add-hook 'scala-mode-hook 'ensime-scala-mode-hook)
```

After adding this and restarting Emacs, you need to actually install ENSIME, which is fortunately really simple. Just use the *M-x package-install* key combination, press *Return*, then enter `ensime`, and press *Return* again. Note that *M* in Emacs stands for the *Alt* key. So the combination is *Alt-x*. However, it is customary to write it the way we did.

Scala integrates well with the SBT tool, which we will discuss in the next section. Instructions on how to integrate the two are given in it. Here we will just list some of the things that ENSIME can do for you to enable you to write code more efficiently and mistake-free. These include code completion, type inspection, automated refactoring, and code navigation. ENSIME will also highlight parts of your code that contain compilation errors. It is usually easy to tell from the markings where you went wrong.

The code completion feature will show you possible completions for the code you are currently typing. If it is a variable name, it will try to guess how to complete it so that you can enter it quickly. Also, you can press the *Tab* key after entering the object name and a dot (.). This will show you a list of all methods you can use for that object.

Type inspection allows you to see what will be the result of Scala's type inference mechanism. To see what type has been inferenced, simply use the *C-c C-v i* key combination. This means *Ctrl-c Ctrl-v i* in Emacs notation.

Automated refactoring features let you conveniently rename variables, without worrying that you may have forgotten some, and do other similar stuff. This is more useful for larger projects.

Code navigation features in ENSIME let you move around in the code by finding the definitions of symbols under the cursor. You can use *M-.* to jump to the definition of the object under the cursor.

The complete command reference for ENSIME can be found at:

```
https://github.com/ensime/ensime-emacs/wiki/Emacs-Command-Reference
```

Profiling Scala code

Profiling Scala code is trickier than one might expect. There are several JVM profilers you can use. However, you will lose some of the Scala abstraction when using them. They are primarily designed for use with Java. These include the VisualVM profiler that can be found at:

```
https://visualvm.java.net/
```

Another possible choice is Takipi, which can be found at the following web address:

```
https://www.takipi.com/
```

Debugging Scala code

Using a dedicated debugger (rather than a bunch of `println` statements) is sometimes the best way of figuring out where you went wrong when writing your program. Debugging is easy when using ENSIME. You can start the debugger with *C-c C-d d*, set a breakpoint on a line that the cursor is on with *C-c C-d b*, or remove a breakpoint with *C-c C-d u*. After you set up your breakpoints, you can start debugging with *C-c C-d r*. After your program stops at a breakpoint, you can use *C-c C-d n* to step to the next line and *C-c C-d i* to inspect the value of the symbol under the cursor. You can use *C-c C-d t* to show the current backtrace. Consult the ENSIME Emacs command reference for a few other important debugger features.

Building, testing, and distributing your Scala software

We are making the assumption that you are familiar with the Scala programming language in this book. Therefore, language concepts are not introduced. We want to present a convenient way of building, testing, and distributing your software. Even if you have already read several books on Scala and implemented some basic (or not so basic) programs, you may still benefit from this.

In this section, we will discuss how to build, test, and distribute your software using the SBT tool. You can get the tool from the SBT website www.scala-sbt.org. There, you will find instructions for how to set it up on whichever operating system you are using. We will only consider here how to use SBT to build and test your software. If you also want to use version control (and you should), then you should consult the documentation and tutorials for tools such as **git**.

SBT is an open source build tool similar to Java's Maven or Ant that lets you compile your Scala project, integrates with many popular Scala test frameworks, has dependency management functionality, integrates with the Scala interpreter, supports mixed Scala/Java projects, and much more.

For this tutorial, we will consider a simple interval arithmetic software package. This will serve as an example to showcase the capabilities of SBT and will also let you try your hand at creating a full (albeit simple) Scala library ready for distribution for other people's benefit. This small package will serve to illustrate the principles of building and testing software with SBT. It is a small library implementing an Interval class and operations that correspond to interval arithmetic for that class.

Interval arithmetic is a generalization of standard arithmetic rules designed to operate on intervals of values. It has many applications in science and engineering. For example, measuring rounding errors or in global optimization methods. While it is full of complex intricacies, at the base of it are some very simple ideas. An interval $[a, b]$ is a range of values between a and b including a and b. Now what is the sum of two intervals $[a, b]$ and $[c, d]$? We will define the sum of two intervals as the interval that the result of adding any number from the interval $[a, b]$ to any number from the interval $[c, d]$ will fall in to. This is simply the interval $[a + c, b + d]$. It is not difficult to convince oneself that this is so by considering that a and c are the smallest numbers from their respective intervals; thus, their sum is the smallest number in the resulting interval. The same goes for the upper bounds b and d.

Similarly for subtraction, we get that $[a, b]$ *minus* $[c, d]$ is equal to $[a - d, b - c]$; for multiplication, we get that $[a, b]$ *times* $[c, d]$ is equal to the interval $[min(ac, ad, bc, bd), max(ac, ad, bc, bd)]$; and finally for division, we get that $[a, b]$ *divided by* $[c, d]$ is equal to $[min(a/c, a/d, b/c, b/d), max(a/c, a/d, b/c, b/d)]$. Finally, we can define the relational operators as follows $[a, b] < [c, d]$ if and only if $b < c$ and similarly $[a, b] > [c, d]$ if and only if $a > d$. Two intervals are considered equal if (and only if) $a = c$ and $b = d$. Using this information lets us define a Scala class called Interval and define operations with the semantics that we discussed here. You should put all of the following code into a file called Interval.scala:

```
package org.intervals.intervals

import java.lang.ArithmeticException
```

```scala
class Interval(ac: Double, bc: Double) {
    var a: Double = ac
    var b: Double = bc
    if (a > b) {
        val tmp = a
        a = b
        b = tmp
    }

    def contains(x: Double): Boolean =
        x >= this.a && x <= this.b

    def contains(x: Interval): Boolean =
        x.a >= this.a && x.b <= this.b

    def +(that: Interval): Interval =
        new Interval(this.a + that.a, this.b + that.b)

    def -(that: Interval): Interval =
        new Interval(this.a - that.b, this.b - that.a)

    def *(that: Interval) : Interval = {
        val all = List(this.a * that.a, this.a * that.b,
                        this.b * that.a, this.b * that.b)
        new Interval(all.min, all.max)
    }

    def /(that: Interval) : Interval = {
        if (that.contains(0.0)) {
            throw new ArithmeticException("Division by an interval
                                    containing zero")
        }
        val all = List(this.a / that.a, this.a / that.b,
                        this.b / that.a, this.b / that.b)
        new Interval(all.min, all.max)
    }

    def ==(that: Interval): Boolean =
        this.a == that.a && this.b == that.b

    def <(that: Interval): Boolean =
        this.b < that.a
```

```
        def >(that: Interval): Boolean =
            this.a > that.b

        override def toString(): String =
            "[" + this.a + ", " + this.b + "]"
    }
```

This will create a new class called `Interval`, which can be constructed by specifying the interval limits. You can then add, subtract, multiply, and divide intervals using standard Scala syntax. We made sure that division by zero threw an exception if the user tries to divide by an interval containing zero. This is because division by zero is undefined, and it is not immediately clear what to do when the interval you divide by contains zero. To use it, you would would use Scala statements such as these:

```
val interval1 = new Interval(-0.5, 0.8)
val interval2 = new Interval(0.3, 0.5)
val interval3 = (interval1 + interval2) * interval3 / (interval1 -
interval2)
```

Obviously, to start doing this, you have to make sure the program using it is able to find it. Let's explore how this can be achieved next.

Directory structure

The SBT tool expects you to follow a certain directory structure that is given here. If you put the appropriate files into specific directories, SBT will be able to automatically build and test your software without having to specify many details in the configuration files:

```
project/
    src/
        main/
            resources/
            scala/
            java/
        test/
            resources/
            scala/
            java/
```

For example, for our project, we will want to create a directory called `intervals` in which we then create the whole directory tree starting with `src`. Naturally, we will want to put our `Interval.scala` file inside the `src/ main/ scala` directory. There is, however, another thing to consider concerning the directory structure. You can follow the Java convention of structuring directories according to the package name. While this is mandatory in Java, it is only optional in Scala, but we will do it anyway. Because of that, our `Interval.scala` file ends up inside the `src/main/scala/org/intervals/intervals` directory.

We now need to tell SBT some basic things about our project. These include various bits of metadata such as the project name, version number, and the version of Scala we want to use. One nice thing about SBT is that it will download the Scala version you need for your project, whichever version you may already have installed on your system. Also, it has to know the root directory of our project. Let's now add the `build.sbt` file to the project. You need to put that file under the `project/` directory of the main project file tree. In our case, we called the project directory `intervals`. For now, fill in the file with the following information:

```
lazy val commonSettings = Seq(
    organization := "org.intervals",
    name := "intervals",
    version := "0.0.1",
    scalaVersion := "2.11.4"
)

lazy val root = (project in file(".")).
    settings(commonSettings: _*)
```

Now, if we want to build the project using SBT, believe it or not nothing remains to be done. SBT will take advantage of the a priori known folder structure and look for files in expected places. Simply go to the `project` directory and issue the following command from the terminal:

```
$ sbt compile console
```

The preceding commands will first compile the Scala code and then put us into the Scala REPL. Alternatively, you can run SBT first and then type the compile and console commands into its command interpreter. After the `Interval.scala` file is compiled, you will be dropped in to the Scala REPL where you can start using your new class immediately. Let's try it out.

We need to import our new library first:

```
scala> import org.intervals.intervals.Interval
import org.intervals.intervals.Interval
```

Now, let's create a couple of `Interval` objects:

```
scala> val ab = new Interval(-3.0, 2.0)
ab: org.intervals.intervals.Interval = [-3.0, 2.0]

scala> val cd = new Interval(4.0, 7.0)
cd: org.intervals.intervals.Interval = [4.0, 7.0]
```

Now, let's test whether our newly defined interval arithmetic operations work as expected:

```
scala> ab + cd
res0: org.intervals.intervals.Interval = [1.0, 9.0]

scala> ab - cd
res1: org.intervals.intervals.Interval = [-10.0, -2.0]

scala> ab * cd
res2: org.intervals.intervals.Interval = [-21.0, 14.0]

scala> ab / cd
res3: org.intervals.intervals.Interval = [-0.75, 0.5]
```

And finally, let's test the relational operators. Again, these will test that our implementation follows the rules we described for partially ordering intervals:

```
scala> ab == cd
res4: Boolean = false

scala> ab < cd
res5: Boolean = true

scala> ab > cd
res6: Boolean = false

scala> ab contains 0.0
res7: Boolean = true
```

It seems that SBT successfully built and loaded our newly created software package. Now, if only there was some way to see if the software works correctly without having to type all that stuff in to the Scala console all the time!

Testing Scala code with the help of SBT

Testing code when you use SBT to build your Scala software is very easy. All you need to do is make sure SBT knows you need the testing framework and then type `sbt compile test` into the command line. To make sure SBT downloads and installs the testing framework of your choice, you need to add it to the `build.sbt` file that we discussed earlier. We recommend using **ScalaTest**, since it allows very simple testing, which is great for medium-sized software that most scientific computing packages are. It also has more advanced capabilities if you need them. To use ScalaTest, add the following line to the end of your `build.sbt` file:

```
libraryDependencies += "org.scalatest" %% "scalatest" % "2.2.0" %
"test"
```

Use a higher version number than 2.2.0 if needed. This will pull in the testing classes as needed. Now, we will need to write the actual test code and put it into our `src/test/scala/` directory. We will be using the appropriately named `FunSuite` class for our tests. Let's call this file `IntervalSuite.scala` and put in the tests that follow. First, we want to import both the `FunSuite` and `Interval` classes, which we will be testing:

```
import org.scalatest.FunSuite
import org.intervals.intervals.Interval

class IntervalSuite extends FunSuite {
```

Testing with `FunSuite` is really simple. Just use `test` followed by description of the test and use `assert` in the body of the test that will fail if our program exhibits undesired behavior. In the following cases, we want to test if our newly defined interval arithmetic operations work according to interval arithmetic rules:

```
test("interval addition should work according to
     interval arithmetic") {
  val interval1 = new Interval(0.1, 0.2)
  val interval2 = new Interval(1.0, 3.0)
  val sum = interval1 + interval2
  assert(sum.a == 1.1)
  assert(sum.b == 3.2)
}

test("interval subtraction should work according to
     interval arithmetic") {
  val interval1 = new Interval(0.1, 0.2)
  val interval2 = new Interval(1.0, 3.0)
  val sub = interval1 - interval2
```

```
      assert(sub.a == -2.9)
      assert(sub.b == -0.8)
  }

  test("inclusion should return true if a Double falls
        within the interval bounds") {
    val interval = new Interval(-1.0, 1.0)
    assert(interval.contains(0.0))
    assert(!interval.contains(2.0))
    assert(!interval.contains(-2.0))
  }

  test("interval multiplication should work according
        to interval arithmetic") {
    val interval1 = new Interval(-2.0, 4.0)
    val interval2 = new Interval(-3.0, -1.0)
    val mul = interval1 * interval2
    assert(mul.a == -12.0)
    assert(mul.b == 6.0)
  }
```

In the following test, we want to test if division works as expected. Division by an interval that contains zero is undefined for our simplified interval arithmetic system. As such, we want the division to signal an exception if the divisor interval contains zero. To do this, we employ the intercept statement. We specify there that we expect that dividing interval2 by interval1 will signal an ArithmeticException exception, which according to our implementation it should:

```
  test("interval division should work according to interval
        arithmetic") {
    val interval1 = new Interval(-2.0, 4.0)
    val interval2 = new Interval(-3.0, -1.0)
    intercept[ArithmeticException] {
      interval2 / interval1
    }
    val div = interval1 / interval2
    assert(div.a == -4.0)
    assert(div.b == 2.0)
  }

  test("equality operator should work according to interval
        arithmetic") {
```

```
    val interval1 = new Interval(-2.0, 4.0)
    assert(interval1 == interval1)
}

test("inequality operators should work according to interval
        arithmetic") {
    val interval1 = new Interval(-2.0, 4.0)
    val interval2 = new Interval(5.0, 6.0)
    assert(interval1 < interval2)
    assert(interval2 > interval1)
    assert(interval1 != interval2)
}
```

Finally, we add one more test to be completely sure. All basic interval arithmetic operations are inclusion-isotonic. This means that, if the intervals are *i1*, *i2*, *i3*, and *i4* and if *i1* is fully contained within *i3* and *i2* is contained within *i4*, then the result of *i1 op i2* is contained within the interval *i3 op i4*. Here, *op* is one of +, -, *, or / defined according to interval arithmetic rules:

```
test("all basic interval arithmetic operations should be
        inclusion isotonic") {
    val interval1 = new Interval(2.0, 4.0)
    val interval2 = new Interval(2.5, 3.5)
    val interval3 = new Interval(1.0, 3.0)
    val interval4 = new Interval(1.5, 2.5)
    assert((interval1 + interval3).contains(interval2 +
            interval3))
    assert((interval1 - interval3).contains(interval2 -
            interval3))
    assert((interval1 * interval3).contains(interval2 *
            interval3))
    assert((interval1 / interval3).contains(interval2 /
            interval3))
}
}
```

With the `IntervalSuite.scala` file put in the `src/ test/ scala` directory, testing our library is simple. Simply type in `sbt compile test` into the console window. The result will show all the tests passed and failed and the reasons for failure if any. Testing your scientific software becomes simple this way: just a matter of writing the tests and using SBT to run them.

ENSIME and SBT integration

You can take advantage of the SBT integration if you use the ENSIME mode for Emacs. To begin using it, you need to create the `.ensime` file in your `project` folder. Do this by adding the following line to your `~/.sbt/0.13/plugins/plugins.sbt` file:

```
addSbtPlugin("org.ensime" % "ensime-sbt" % "0.2.0")
```

Now, you can just go to the root of your `project` folder and issue the `sbt gen-ensime` command. This will create the `.ensime` file using the information gathered by SBT about your project. After that, you can start using ENSIME to develop your project. Just load the newly created `.ensime` file before starting ENSIME.

Distributing your software

After you have written your oh-so-useful Scala library, you will probably want other people be able to use it. Ideally, you just want people to append the library name to their library dependencies list in the `build.sbt` file and then have that package automatically downloaded whenever needed. The process for publishing software this way is not currently very simple. There is, however, a simpler way of publishing your software and that is as an unmanaged dependency. Unmanaged dependencies differ from managed ones. The user will have to download a `.jar` file containing your library and place it under the `lib` directory in their project file tree in an unmanaged dependency. To create a `.jar` file for your project, all you have to do is use the `sbt publish` command. Simply type in `sbt publish` at the console and your Scala package will be compiled and put in `target/ intervals_2.11-0.0.1.jar`. Now, it is a simple matter of putting that `.jar` file in the `lib/ directory` of the project you want to use it in. Alternatively, you can put it up online for people to download. One thing to watch out for though is that, if your library has dependencies, then the user of that library will have to make sure they also end up in their `lib/` folder.

Now, let's test this with our intervals library. First package it using the `sbt publish` command. Then, create a new project. It is actually very simple. Instead of creating a full project tree, you can simply create a directory for the project and put your source code directly in it. SBT is clever enough to figure out what is going on in these cases too.

Let's say we create a new project directory called `intervals_user`; inside this directory, create a new directory called `lib`. Now, copy the result of the `sbt publish` command, which will be called `intervals_2.11-0.0.1.jar` and will reside in the target subdirectory of our intervals project to this new directory. From here on, SBT will let you use this library in your new project. Create a new file called `IntervalUser.scala` and put the following code there:

```scala
import org.orbitfold.iafs.Interval

object IntervalUser {
  def main(args: Array[String]) = {
    val interval1 = new Interval(-0.5, 0.5)
    val interval2 = new Interval(0.2, 0.8)
    println(interval1 + interval2)
    println(interval1 - interval2)
    println(interval1 * interval2)
    println(interval1 / interval2)
  }
}
```

It is now simple to run this program. You can merely issue the `sbt run` command in the `intervals_user` folder that we created for this project. If you have done everything right, you should see the following lines as part of the output of this program:

```
[-0.3, 1.3]
[-1.3, 0.3]
[-0.4, 0.4]
[-2.5, 2.5]
```

Another method for distributing software is more involved. SBT uses Apache Ivy, which in turn looks for packages on the central Maven repository by default. What happens when you add a dependency to the library dependencies list in your `build.sbt` file is that the information there is used to locate the appropriate files on the Maven repository; the files are then downloaded to your computer. The process of publishing your library to these is complicated and will not be discussed here since it would be a large detour for a book about writing scientific software with Scala. For now, you can simply ask people to download your package to their `lib` folder. After you have worked more on your library and want it known and widely used, you can look up the process for publishing software to Maven central online.

Mixing Java and Scala code

Using Java code from Scala is fairly easy. This is because both languages are based on JVM. Using Scala code in Java is also possible but trickier. In general, Scala is designed to be compatible with Java. You can take advantage of this if you want to use one of the many available Java libraries. For example, you could use Java's Swing library to write a user interface for your program, or you may want to use Java's useful JFreeChart to perform data visualization or just basic plotting. All Java concepts translate more or less directly to the Scala concepts. We will look into that in one of the chapters of this book. For now, let's consider a really simple Scala program just to see how easy it is to write user interfaces with Swing in Scala. You can type the following into a script and then run it on Unix-like systems. You may have to modify the shell name and parameters:

```
#!/bin/sh
exec scala "$0" "$@"
!#

import javax.swing.JFrame

object GUIHelloWorld extends App {
  val f = new JFrame
  f.setVisible(true)
  f.setTitle("Hello, world!")
  f.setSize(300, 200)
  f.setDefaultCloseOperation(JFrame.EXIT_ON_CLOSE)
}

HelloWorld.main(args)
```

We will discuss using other Java libraries in *Chapter 8, Scientific Plotting with Scala*.

Summary

In this chapter, we discussed the advantages of using Scala over other programming languages and environments for scientific computing. These include static typing and strong support for functional programming. We discussed how this will help you write better scientific software. We compared Scala to other popular programming languages and discussed their comparative merits and demerits; that is, Scala will allow you to write faster, better structured software while also keeping most of the advantages of dynamic languages.

We had a quick overview of the major scientific packages available for use in Scala. These cover a range from linear algebra and data analysis to statistical modeling. Using the ENSIME mode for Emacs and other text editors as a Scala IDE was discussed; we have also shown how to use ENSIME when debugging Scala code. Finally, and perhaps most importantly, we showed you how to use SBT to package, build, test, and distribute your software. Using well-established, convenient, and powerful build tools is very important since it removes a lot of the chores from writing software and allows you to concentrate on what is important.

We guided you through the process of writing, building, testing, and distributing an example library written in Scala. After all, you probably want your software to be used by other people. We also briefly describe how one would use Java libraries from a Scala program. You will want to know this since you will probably want your standalone program to have a nice Swing interface, or you could take advantage of JFreeChart when performing scientific plotting.

Downloading the example code

You can download the example code files for this book from your account at http://www.packtpub.com. If you purchased this book elsewhere, you can visit http://www.packtpub.com/support and register to have the files e-mailed directly to you.

- You can download the code files by following these steps:
- Log in or register to our website using your e-mail address and password.
- Hover the mouse pointer on the SUPPORT tab at the top.
- Click on Code Downloads & Errata.
- Enter the name of the book in the Search box.
- Select the book for which you're looking to download the code files.
- Choose from the drop-down menu where you purchased this book from.
- Click on Code Download.

You can also download the code files by clicking on the Code Files button on the book's webpage at the Packt Publishing website. This page can be accessed by entering the book's name in the Search box. Please note that you need to be logged in to your Packt account.

Once the file is downloaded, please make sure that you unzip or extract the folder using the latest version of:

- WinRAR / 7-Zip for Windows
- Zipeg / iZip / UnRarX for Mac
- 7-Zip / PeaZip for Linux

2
Storing and Retrieving Data

In this chapter, we will discuss data storage and retrieval in Scala. These two things are important to know about, because in most contexts you will need to perform anything that could be considered scientific computing. You will very likely need to read in data in some format and to output the results in some format. For example, a lot of test data for pattern recognition algorithms is stored in CSV format. Another popular way of storing data is in SQL databases. For use in any kind of numerical or symbolic calculations, this data will have to be retrieved. To retrieve it, you must have a way of writing SQL queries to be performed on the said database. Another popular way to store data, especially if the data is large in volume, is HDF5 format files. They are commonly used to store the results of experiments producing large amounts of data that need to be stored in a structured way. Whenever possible, we will try to present the best possible way of handling these file formats in Scala. By the end of this chapter, you will be storing and retrieving your data conveniently and quickly. We will cover the following topics in this chapter:

- Reading and writing CSV files
- Reading and writing JSON files
- Reading and writing XML files
- Database access using JDBC
- Database access using Slick
- Reading and writing HDF5 files

Reading and writing CSV files

We will examine reading and writing CSV files here. **CSV** stands for **Comma Separated Values**. These files are just records arranged in rows with a row consisting of multiple values separated by commas (and sometimes other separator symbols, such as spaces or tabs). Instead of relying on ready-made libraries to do this, we will write our own small, extensible class for reading and writing data in CSV format.

The reason for this is that the file format is so simple it requires little more effort than reading a text file line by line. Therefore, the resulting code is simple, short, and will save you an extra dependency. Also, there does not seem to be a de facto standard for CSV access in Scala. It will serve us as an introduction to file access in Scala, which may come in handy if you need to read other weird file formats. Here is an example of a CSV file containing a part of the famous IRIS dataset. It is very commonly used to sanity test pattern recognition and classification algorithms. Also for multivariate data visualization and any other task, a very simple, fairly low dimensional dataset is required with easily separable classes of objects.

Each row in a file represents measurements of an Iris flower. These are: sepal length in centimeters, sepal width in centimeters, petal length in centimeters, petal width in centimeters, and the name of the flower that was being measured, in that order. For classification methods, the task is to learn to recognize the species of the plant from these measurements:

```
5.1,3.5,1.4,0.2,Iris-setosa
4.9,3.0,1.4,0.2,Iris-setosa
4.7,3.2,1.3,0.2,Iris-setosa
4.6,3.1,1.5,0.2,Iris-setosa
5.0,3.6,1.4,0.2,Iris-setosa
5.4,3.9,1.7,0.4,Iris-setosa
4.6,3.4,1.4,0.3,Iris-setosa
```

You can get this dataset from the *UCI Machine Learning Repository* website, which houses data files for many different datasets. Most of these are in CSV format. If you want to read them, you will need to understand the lessons in this chapter! The link to the dataset is `https://archive.ics.uci.edu/ml/datasets/Iris`.

Retrieve the dataset from there, since we will use it to test the code we develop in the following sections. For this, you will want to create a simple SBT project. In *Chapter 1, Introducing Scientific Computing with Scala*, we saw how to use SBT to build complete projects. However, you can use SBT in a much simpler way, without creating a whole project tree. For now, simply create a new folder called `csvreader` and a file in it called `CSVReader.scala`. Now, put the following code in that file:

```
object HelloWorld {
  def main(args: Array[String]) {
    println("I will read CSV files soon!")
  }
}
```

Now, running the program in this file is simply a question of typing in the sbt run command in the command line. If you have done everything properly and installed the SBT tool that was discussed in *Chapter 1, Introducing Scientific Computing with Scala*, it should print a line of text as follows:

```
[info] Compiling 1 Scala source to /home/vytas/csvreader/target/
scala-2.10/classes...
[info] Running HelloWorld
I will read CSV files soon!
[success] Total time: 4 s, completed Sep 16, 2015 10:36:31 PM
```

This is a very neat feature of SBT that allows you to quickly write simple scripts you want to test without setting up the complete build environment you might need with other compiled languages. We will take advantage of this when discussing other topics as well. Now on to actually reading CSV files; download and put the IRIS dataset in the directory you have your script in.

Reading files in Scala

Knowing how to read simple text files is often a very useful thing for unstructured text formats such as CSV. Usually, it is most convenient to simply read the file line by line and then process the lines. In the following code sample, we will see how to print a file line by line. You would simply substitute println with the text processing code you need. For now, we will simply print it as follows:

```
import scala.io.Source

object CSVReader {
    def main(args: Array[String]) {
        for (line <- Source.fromFile("iris.csv").getLines()) {
            println(line)
        }
    }
}
```

The following is the beginning of the output that should be the result of running this program:

```
5.1,3.5,1.4,0.2,Iris-setosa
4.9,3.0,1.4,0.2,Iris-setosa
4.7,3.2,1.3,0.2,Iris-setosa
4.6,3.1,1.5,0.2,Iris-setosa
5.0,3.6,1.4,0.2,Iris-setosa
...
```

Just make sure you have called the file with the IRIS data `iris.csv` for this to work. Otherwise, it will throw an exception. Alternatively, you can use any text file to test this bit of code. The preceding code works; however, there is a problem with it. It will leave the file opened. While this may be okay for short scripts it is suboptimal for larger applications. In order to avoid this, you can use another approach. A simple way of doing this is to use Java's `FileReader` class. An example of doing it this way is given here. This is far less elegant than the idiomatic way, but has the advantage of working correctly:

```
import java.io.{FileReader, BufferedReader}

object CSVReader {
  def main(args: Array[String]) {
    val file = new FileReader("iris.csv")
    val reader = new BufferedReader(file)
    try {
      var line:String = null
      while ({line = reader.readLine(); line} != null) {
        println(line)
      }
    }
    finally {
      reader.close()
    }
  }
}
```

You should test both of these on the IRIS dataset or any other text file you have lying around. They should both produce the same result, with the difference being that the second version closes the file after it is done with it. It is more or less a direct conversion of a similar Java program.

Parsing CSV data

Parsing the lines in a CSV file is simple. What we probably want to do is cut the lines up using a specified delimiter (usually a comma, space, or a tab). Since files sometimes use different delimiters, we will want to let the user specify which one to use, with comma being the default. We will also want to remove the white space to each side of the newly split word. This is because it might contain extra characters that we don't need if people use more than one space to separate values, for example, or leave spaces around commas. The `trim` method gets rid of white space at the beginning and end of a string. All of this can be accomplished by a single line:

```
val delimiterg = ","
line.split(delimiter).map(_.trim)
```

This will return an array of strings with values as elements. These values are, of course, all strings now. We probably will want to do some kind of inference to see if values in the CSV files are meant to be numerical or symbolic. Alternatively, this can be left to the user with knowledge of the CSV row format.

Processing CSV data

Now, let's collect the data we obtained after splitting the string. A Scala Map is a good candidate for a structure to store this data in. We will want the keys to be the names of the columns in the IRIS dataset. The values will then be the columns themselves. The following is given a mutable Map definition that we will use to store this data:

```
import scala.collection.mutable.Map
val csvdata: Map[List[String]] = new Map[List[String]]
```

Now to fill it in we have the following program:

```
import scala.collection.mutable.{MutableList, Map}
import java.io.{FileReader, BufferedReader}

object CSVReader {
  def main(args: Array[String]) {
    val file = new FileReader("iris.csv")
    val reader = new BufferedReader(file)
    try {
      val alldata = new MutableList[Array[String]]
      var line:String = null
      while ({line = reader.readLine(); line} != null) {
        if (line.length != 0) {
          val delimiter: String = ","
```

```
                var splitline: Array[String] =
                line.split(delimiter).map(_.trim)
                alldata += splitline
            }
        }
        val labels = MutableList("sepal length", "sepal width",
        // 1
            "petal length", "petal width", "class")
        val labelled = labels.zipWithIndex.map {
            case (label, index) => label -> alldata.map(x => x(index))
            // 2
        }
        val csvdata: Map[String, MutableList[String]] = Map()
        for (pair <- labelled) {
            csvdata += pair // 3
        }
    }
    finally {
        reader.close()
    }
    }
}
```

In the line labeled in the comment as 1, we define the labels that the columns of the CSV file will take. This we will leave to the user. CSV files have no standard way of naming columns. In the bit of code named 2, in the comment, we extract the column from the area of prepared CSV value rows. Finally, we stuff it all in to a Scala Map. Now, all we have to do is build on this and construct and test the CSVReader class.

Reading and writing JSON files

JavaScript Object Notation (JSON) files are a common way of serializing data. It was proposed by Douglas Crockford and is described in the RFC 7159 standard. In particular, they are good at storing complex data structures such as dictionaries. Many languages have strong libraries for JSON support. It is very common to store your program data in JSON files. It is a good format in which to save files and the like. It is also commonly used for storing input data for various simulation programs. It is far more human-readable and -writable than XML and has largely replaced it in some uses. For example, it has largely replaced XML in asynchronous browser/ server communication. We will look into several libraries that you can use to access JSON files in Scala.

Here's a small tip for using some third-party libraries. If you download them from GitHub or some other source code repository and the project uses SBT, then the easiest way to use them in your software is to simply use the `sbt package` command and then copy the resulting `.jar` file to the `lib` folder of your SBT project. Alternatively, you can consult the instructions provided by the maintainers of the package. Some packages will be available as downloadable dependencies to be added to the `build.sbt` file.

We will use the small JSON file provided here to test the libraries discussed in this section. It is a simple example containing some details about some of the planets in our solar system. The values in question were taken from Wikipedia:

```
{
    "gasGiants": [
    {
        "name" : "Jupiter",
            "satellites": [
                "Ganymede",
                "Callisto",
                "Io",
                "Europa"
            ],
            "mass": 1.8986e+27
        },
        {
        "name": "Saturn",
            "satellites": [
                "Mimas",
                "Enceladus",
                "Tethys",
                "Dione"
            ],
            "mass": 5.683e+26
        }
    ],
    "rockyPlanets": [
        {
        "name" : "Earth",
            "satellites": [
                "Moon"
            ],
            "mass": 5.972e+24
        },
        {
```

```
        "name" : "Mars",
            "satellites": [
                "Phobos",
                "Deimos"
            ],
            "mass": 6.39e+23
        }
    ]
}
```

 You can use an online JSON validator if you want to make sure this is a valid JSON file. An excellent one is available at the following link: http://jsonlint.com/

Save the JSON data as `planets.json` or some other filename in a new folder that you will use to test the code. We will again be using SBT in the same way as in the previous section. Just create a new folder, put your `.scala` file in it, and then perform `sbt run` when you want to run it. Whenever possible, download the libraries in the question, perform `sbt package`, and put the resulting `.jars` in the `lib` folder under the folder your code is in. As everywhere else in this book, we will try to pick libraries with some staying power but it is not clear at this point what will become the dominant approach to handling JSON in Scala. Most of the principles, however, should remain the same no matter what library you are using.

Spray-JSON

Spray-JSON is taken from the Spray framework for building RESTful web services. It is part of Spray, but can be downloaded and used independently of it. You can get it from the following link at https://github.com/spray/spray-json.

Just use Git to obtain the source code, and then build it with the `sbt` package. After it is done building, copy the resulting `target/scala/spray-json_...jar` file to the `lib` directory of the directory containing your test script. Create a file called `SprayTest.scala` and put the following code in there. Note that it is very important that your project uses the same Scala version as the one that was used to build Spray-JSON. To make sure that is the case look at the `build.sbt` file of the Spray-JSON project. Let's say it contains the following line:

```
scalaVersion := "2.11.6"
```

In that case, it is best to make sure your project also uses this version; otherwise, your project may be incompatible with the library. In this case, you may want to create a simple build.sbt file in the directory that contains the SprayTest.scala file.

At first, we will want to define case classes to which we will convert the JSON **Abstract Syntax Tree (AST)** representation that Spray-JSON uses. In our case, it is defined by the following three case classes:

```
case class Planet(name: String, satellites: Array[String], mass:
Float)
case class Planets(gassGiants: Array[Planet], rockyPlanets:
Array[Planet])
```

In our case, a planet consists of a satellite's name, an array of satellite names, and its mass. Finally, planets are arranged into two major types. One is gas giants and the other is rocky planets. We want case classes to reflect that. In case the reader has forgotten what case classes are, we give a short explanation here:

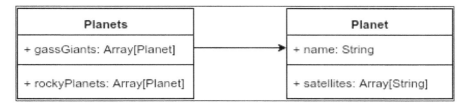

The case classes are a kind of convenience feature in Scala. They can be incredibly useful when used with pattern matching. Simply put, a case class is simply a class with a case modifier. The modifier makes the compiler add some convenient methods to the class. For example, you don't need to use the new keyword when creating instances of the class; it implements string representation methods and some others. More importantly, you can access the constructor parameters. This is useful when you want to define record type structures. For example, a description of a person with name, age, and so on, to be used more as data than as a more traditional object would be implemented naturally as a case class. You can try the following commands in the Scala REPL:

```
scala> case class Person(name: String, age: Int, occupation: String)
defined class Person

scala> val bob = Person("Bob", 30, "Baker")
bob: Person = Person(Bob,30,Baker)

scala> val anna = Person("Anna", 25, "Lawyer")
```

```
anna: Person = Person(Anna,25,Lawyer)

scala> bob.name
res2: String = Bob

scala> anna.age
res3: Int = 25
```

It should be obvious that the case classes are a fairly natural way of viewing the type of data records that are usually stored in JSON files. As such, we will use them for accessing data stored in our JSON file:

```
import spray.json._
import DefaultJsonProtocol._

case class Planet(name: String, satellites: List[String], mass:
Float)
case class Planets(gasGiants: List[Planet], rockyPlanets:
List[Planet])

object PlanetsJsonProtocol extends DefaultJsonProtocol {
  implicit val planetFormat = jsonFormat(Planet, "name",
  "satellites", "mass")
  implicit val planetsFormat = jsonFormat(Planets, "gasGiants",
  "rockyPlanets")
}

import PlanetsJsonProtocol.{planetFormat, planetsFormat_

object SprayReader {
    def main(args: Array[String]) {
      val rawText =
      scala.io.Source.fromFile("planets.json").mkString
      val jsonAst = rawText.parseJson
      val planets = jsonAst.convertTo[Planets]
      println(planets.gasGiants(0).name)
      println(planets.rockyPlanets(1).satellites)
    }
}
```

This program, if run, will print out the following two lines:

```
Jupiter
List(Phobos, Deimos)
```

To the reader more used to dynamically typed languages, this seems like a lot of work. However, what you get is not only simple JSON parsing, but also JSON validation and a kind of JSON schema checking. It will only allow you to load JSON files that follow the defined format. This may seem strict, but such is the way of statically typed languages. After using the `convertTo[Planets]` method, you can simply proceed to access the data as you would if it was simply stored in members of the `case` class instance, which it is. Were the `case` class and JSON object to have nonmatching fields, a runtime error would occur specifying the fields causing the problem. The conversion is achieved by extending the `DefaultJsonProtocol` class. The `jsonFormat` method is used with the `case` classes to define rules for how the abstract syntax class will be parsed in to Scala objects. In this case, we simply specify our `case` classes and define the JSON property names. The names have to match those in the file. The property names will be taken in the order they are specified in the `jsonFormat` method and used to construct an instance of the `case` class. It also goes the other way. Using the same `PlanetsJsonProtocol` class, we can convert an instance of the `case` classes into a JSON abstract syntax tree. An example of this is given here:

```
val planets = jsonAst.convertTo[Planets]
val json = planets.toJson.prettyPrint
```

The second line will convert the `case` class instance to a JSON AST and then to a string that you can then write back to a JSON file. Here is a small example of how you would do this with a different, simpler data structure:

```
import spray.json._
import DefaultJsonProtocol._
import java.io._

case class Person(name: String, age: Int, occupation: String)

object PersonJsonProtocol extends DefaultJsonProtocol {
  implicit val personFormat = jsonFormat(Person, "name", "age",
  "occupation")
}

import PersonJsonProtocol._

object SprayWriter {
  def main(args: Array[String]) {
    val bob = Person("Bob", 30, "Baker")
    val pw = new PrintWriter(new File("person.json"))
    pw.write(bob.toJson.prettyPrint)
    pw.close()
  }
}
```

This program creates an instance of a `case` class, converts it to a JSON AST, and writes it to a file called `person.json`. Other than the writing bits, everything else is the same as in our previous example. To understand the capabilities and other features of this library one will have to look at the source as the documentation is currently very basic. The contents of the file we created by running the preceding program should be as follows:

```
{
    "name": "Bob",
    "age": 30,
    "occupation": "Baker"
}
```

SON of JSON

The SON of JSON library can be found at the following link:

```
https://github.com/wspringer/sonofjson
```

This is a completely different approach from the Spray-JSON library we considered previously. Using it feels more like using a JSON library in a dynamic language such as Python. It is very simple to use and can be great if you just need something quick and dirty to put in a throw-away script.

The following code will read our `planets.json` file. As you can see, the boilerplate code when using this library is reduced to the bare minimum. On the flip side, you cannot use it to check if the JSON file being read is in the correct format:

```scala
import nl.typeset.sonofjson._

object SonOfJson {
  def main(args: Array[String]) {
    val rawText =
    scala.io.Source.fromFile("planets.json").mkString
    val planets = parse(rawText)
    println(planets)
  }
}
```

When run, it will print the following:

```
JObject(Map(rockyPlanets -> JArray(ArrayBuffer(JObject(Map(mass ->
JNumber(5.972E+24), name -> JString(Earth), satellites -> JArray(Array
Buffer(JString(Moon))))), JObject(Map(mass -> JNumber(6.39E+23), name
-> JString(Mars), satellites -> JArray(ArrayBuffer(JString(Phobos),
JString(Deimos)))))))), gasGiants -> JArray(ArrayBuffer(JObject(Map(ma
ss -> JNumber(1.8986E+27), name -> JString(Jupiter), satellites -> JA
rray(ArrayBuffer(JString(Ganymede), JString(Callisto), JString(Io),
JString(Europa))))), JObject(Map(mass -> JNumber(5.683E+26), name
-> JString(Saturn), satellites -> JArray(ArrayBuffer(JString(Mimas),
JString(Enceladus), JString(Tethys), Jstring(Dione))))))))))
```

This is the internal representation used by the library to store the data from the JSON file. As can be seen, it feels almost transparent. All the data is stored as a `case` class instances, and the types of object are sensibly chosen to represent the types of data stored in the file.

The following example would print `Moon` if planets were the value containing the preceding object:

```
println(planets.rockyPlanets.Earth.satellites(0))
```

Argonaut

Argonaut takes a purely functional approach to parsing JSON files. It is different from the preceding two libraries. As such, it will serve as a good third example of how you can use JSON from your software. You can find the library at the following link:

```
http://argonaut.io/
```

After adding it to your `build.sbt` file, as a library dependency, you can begin using it. First, we need to import the libraries. The library itself requires a bit more boilerplate than SON of JSON. To read the data, we need to first define the `case` classes. For our example, they are again as given here:

```
import argonaut._, Argonaut._

case class Planet(name: String, satellites: List[String], mass:
Float)
case class Planets(gasGiants: List[Planet], rockyPlanets:
List[Planet])
```

After that we will define codecs and parse our JSON file:

```
object Planet {
  implicit def PlanetCodecJson: CodecJson[Planet] =
```

```
      casecodec3(Planet.apply, Planet.unapply)("name", "satellites",
      "mass")
  }

  object Planets {
    implicit def PlanetsCodecJson: CodecJson[Planets] =
      casecodec2(Planets.apply, Planets.unapply)("gasGiants",
      "rockyPlanets")
  }

  object ArgonautTest {
    def main(args: Array[String]) {
      val rawText =
      scala.io.Source.fromFile("planets.json").mkString
      val planets = rawText.decode[Planets]
      println(planets)
    }
  }
```

For more elaborate uses of this library, refer to the documentation. As opposed to most Scala projects, this one has decent documentation. It can be found at the following link:

```
http://argonaut.io/doc/
```

Reading and writing XML files

XML or **Extensible Markup Language** is a popular markup language. It was designed to be both human- and machine-readable, but with an apparent emphasis on the later. XML is very widely supported and commonly used for file formats of various programs. For example, the popular Open Document Format is XML-based. The popularity of XML is mostly due to its historical use and support. It is often replaced by lighter languages such as JSON because of XML's relative verbosity and complexity. We will assume that the reader has a basic working knowledge of XML. However, to recap the basics, XML consists of **tags** and **text**. Tags are the start and end varieties. Start tags look like this: `<tag>`, while end tags look like this: `</tag>`. Usually a value in XML is encoded as such: `<name>Bob</name>`, with a property name as the tag name and its value being the text between the tags. The data between two XML tags can be any valid XML. We will see a more complicated example later.

Luckily for us, XML support is built-in to Scala. Because of this we will not have to dig in to third-party libraries. In fact XML support in Scala is fairly extensive. For example you can simply write XML data wherever an expression is expected. Try the following in the REPL:

```
scala> val person = <person>
     | <name>Bob</name>
     | <age>30</age>
     | <occupation>Baker</occupation>
     | </person>
person: scala.xml.Elem =
<person>
<name>Bob</name>
<age>30</age>
<occupation>Baker</occupation>
</person>
```

You can obviously do the same inside any Scala program or script. Any XML expression will be instantly parsed into an appropriate object. Let's go through an example using Scala's XML features using the planet example we used for JSON earlier. Put the code into the `ScalaXml.scala` file and compile/run it with `sbt` as we did before.

First, we defined a class called `Planet`. In this class, we defined several members representing information about a planet. To get its XML representation, we will simply overload its `toXML` method. This method will return an XML expression containing data we want in it. An important point here is that you can execute arbitrary code inside an XML expression by surrounding it in curly braces. The code inside the curly braces may itself contain an XML expression; therefore, it may be the case that these braces get nested. It is indeed the case in the following `Planet` class. We want to iterate satellites over the planet and surround their names by the `<satellite>...</satellite>` tag pair. To get the name, we use nested curly braces:

```
class Planet {
  val name: String
  val satellites: List[String]
  val mass: Double

  def toXML =
    <planet>
      <name>{name}</name>
      <satellites>{ satellites.map(satellite =>
        <satellite>
          { satellite }
        </satellite>) }
      </satellites>
```

```
            <mass>{mass}</mass>
        </planet>
    }
```

The `Planets` class and its `toXML` method are an example of how you can perform nested XML structures this way. The `Planets` class's structure has two properties consisting of a list of planets. We call each planet's `toXML` method inside the curly braces to get its XML representation. This representation then becomes part of the `Planets` XML representation:

```
class Planets {
  val gasGiants: List[Planet]
  val rockyPlanets: List[Planet]

  def toXML =
    <planets>
      <gasGiants>
        { gasGiants.map(planet =>
          planet.toXML) }
      </gasGiants>
      <rockyPlanets>
        { rockyPlanets.map(planet =>
          planet.toXML) }
      </rockyPlanets>
    </planets>
}
```

Finally, we can test it by creating instances of our classes and calling `toXML` on them. This is done in the following code sample. The code should print out an XML representation of the `planets` object:

```
object XMLTest {
  def main(args: Array[String]) {
    val jupiter = new Planet {
      val name = "Jupiter"
      val satellites = List("Ganymede", "Callisto",
        "Io", "Europa")
      val mass = 1.8986e+27
    }
    val saturn = new Planet {
      val name = "Saturn"
      val satellites = List("Mimas", "Enceladus",
        "Tethys", "Dione")
      val mass = 5.683e+26
    }
```

```
    val earth = new Planet {
      val name = "Earth"
      val satellites = List("Moon")
      val mass = 5.972e+24
    }
    val mars = new Planet {
      val name = "Mars"
      val satellites = List("Phobos", "Deimos")
      val mass = 6.39e+23
    }
    val planets = new Planets {
      val gasGiants = List(jupiter, saturn)
      val rockyPlanets = List(earth, mars)
    }
    println(planets.toXML)
  }
}
```

This is straightforward enough. The remaining two topics we want to cover are accessing the members of XML data structures and reading/writing XML files. The former allows us to access data stored in XML files while the latter allows us to read and write XML files ourselves.

There is a convenient syntax for querying XML data structures. If we want to find out, for example, the mass of Jupiter, we can use the following lines:

```
val planetsxml = planets.toXML
val gasGiantNodes = planetsxml \ "gasGiants" \ "planet"
val planetJupiter =
  gasGiantNodes.filter(planet =>
    ((planet \ "name").text == "Jupiter"))
println((planetJupiter \ "mass").text)
```

Here, the \ method is used to extract the subelements of a given XML structure. We need to extract them in this sequence to reach the mass of Jupiter. First, we get all the gas giants and store them as gasGiantNodes. Then, we look for one whose name is Jupiter and then extract its mass.

One remaining point is using XML attributes. Each tag can get a number of attributes in XML. For example, see the following tags:

```
val bob = <person name="Bob" age="30" occupation="Baker"></person>
```

To extract the attributes from a tag like this, you can use the \ method. Just add a @ sign to it. For example, you can perform the following to extract Bob's age:

```
bob \ "@age"
```

You can combine these different operators to extract information from the XML files. You should also consult the official documentation for the XML classes whenever information here proves to be insufficient for your cause.

Saving and loading XML files is very easy. You can convert XML data to a string using the `toString` method. For example, the following will return a string representation of our planets data.

```
planets.toString
```

This is, however, not necessary for saving and loading files. You can simply use convenient methods provided by Scala specifically for this purpose. Just do the following for writing the planets data to a file:

```
scala.xml.XML.save("planets.xml", planets)
```

And the following to read the planets data back from the file:

```
val node = scala.xml.XML.loadFile("planets.xml")
```

This concludes our discussion of Scala's XML processing capabilities, which are quite impressive. If you have further questions, you should consult Scala's official documentation.

Database access using JDBC

In relational databases, data is organized in to tables with multiple columns and rows where each row gets a unique key. Columns usually represent properties while rows represent different objects or data records. Relational databases were proposed by E. F. Codd in the 1970's. They are a popular way of storing all kinds of data. Usually, relation database systems provide fast and convenient access to data using various queries. These queries describe various conditions that have to be satisfied by the data being retrieved. This allows one to select and combine database rows to retrieve information. Virtually all relational database systems use SQL to query and maintain the database. You can use SQL statements to insert data into database, create new tables, drop tables, query data, and perform other tasks. JDBC is Java's standard for connecting to databases and executing SQL statements. One straightforward way of accessing relational databases from Scala is using the JDBC library that Java provides. We will see how to do this using a SQLite database. However, the principles explained here will also apply to any other relational database management system.

To run the following examples, you will need to get JDBC drivers for SQLite from the following repository and put them in the `lib` folder of your project:

`https://bitbucket.org/xerial/sqlite-jdbc/downloads`

The following program will connect to a SQLite database via JDBC. You can then use the connection object to execute SQL statements:

```
import java.sql.DriverManager
import java.sql.Connection

object JdbcSqlite {
  def main(args: Array[String]) {
    var c: Connection = null
    try {
      Class.forName("org.sqlite.JDBC")
      c = DriverManager.getConnection
      ("jdbc:sqlite:planets.sqlite")
    } catch {
      case e: Throwable => e.printStackTrace
    }
    c.close()
  }
}
```

First, we import the JDBC classes needed to create a connection. These are `DriverManager` and `Connection`. We will use an instance of the `Collection` class to represent a connection to our database. It is in using this object that we will be executing SQL statements. The `Class.forName("org.sqlite.JDBC")` statement returns an object associated with the class `org.sqlite.JDBC`. This was the standard way, in the JDBC world, to make sure that the required JDBC drivers are loaded. However, since JDBC 4.0, you can omit this statement. Since it does no harm and slightly improves backwards compatibility, we will leave it. Then, we try to establish a connection with the database. This is done using the `getConnection` method. The argument to this method is the URL specific to the relational database management system used. In our case, it specifies that we will be using SQLite and the name of the file we will use to store our database in. In other cases, it might consist of an IP address and port used to access the database server.

A new database will be created when the program above is run. To create the tables, we will use the `Connection` object. Obviously, you can also create the tables using the command-line tools or GUI that your database management system provides. We will create a simple table for the planets. You need to insert the code right after the invocation of the `getConnection` method in the preceding skeletal JDBC program. Alternatively, you can do it from the Scala REPL:

```
val s = c.createStatement()
s.executeUpdate("""CREATE TABLE planet(
                ID INT PRIMARY KEY NOT NULL,
                NAME TEXT NOT NULL,
                MASS REAL NOT NULL,
                PERIOD REAL NOT NULL);""")
```

Now, we will want to populate the table with some entries. The point of this is so that we can show how to handle retrieving data from databases in Scala. We will not examine the finer points of SQL here. You are encouraged to consult books on SQL if you need a refresher:

```
s.executeUpdate("""INSERT INTO planet
                VALUES (0, "Mercury", 3.3011E23, 0.240864)""")
s.executeUpdate("""INSERT INTO planet
                VALUES (1, "Venus", 4.8675E24, 0.615)""")
s.executeUpdate("""INSERT INTO planet
                VALUES (2, "Earth", 5.97237E24, 1)""")
s.executeUpdate("""INSERT INTO planet
                VALUES (3, "Mars", 6.4171E23, 1.881)""")
s.executeUpdate("""INSERT INTO planet
                VALUES (4, "Jupiter", 1.8986E27, 11.86)""")
s.executeUpdate("""INSERT INTO planet
                VALUES (5, "Saturn", 5.6836E26, 29.46)""")
s.executeUpdate("""INSERT INTO planet
                VALUES (6, "Uranus", 8.6810E25, 84.01)""")
s.executeUpdate("""INSERT INTO planet
                VALUES (7, "Neptune", 1.0243E26, 164.8)""")
```

This will insert the planet information in to our `planet` table in the newly created database. Now if we want to select, for example, all the planets with a mass larger than Earth, we can use the following query (you will have to import `ResultSet` from `java.sql`):

```
val query = """select * from planet where mass >
  (select mass from planet where name="Earth")"""
val rs: ResultSet = s.executeQuery(query)
while (rs.next()) {
```

```
val name = rs.getString("name")
val mass = rs.getFloat("mass")
println(name + " " + mass)
}
```

The preceding code will select those planets with a mass greater than Earth's. It will then loop through the results set and print the planet's name and mass. You can similarly construct more complicated queries. Analyzing the results is just a matter of looping over the `ResultSet` object and extracting the fields you need.

Database access using Slick

Slick or **Scala Language-Integrated Connection Kit** (apparently) is a **Functional Relational Mapping** (**FRM**) library for Scala that makes it possible to work with relational databases using abstractions natural to the Scala language. The library is developed by Typesafe, which is the company founded by Scala's creator Martin Odersky. Working with the library makes working with databases similar to working with Scala's Collections API. The library can be found at the following website:

```
http://slick.typesafe.com/
```

To install the library with `sbt`, you should add the following to the `build.sbt` file library dependencies:

```
libraryDependencies ++= Seq(
  "com.typesafe.slick" %% "slick" % "3.0.3",
  "org.slf4j" % "slf4j-nop" % "1.6.4"
)
```

Plain SQL

Slick supports Plain SQL queries. This basically means that you can write your queries in straight SQL without having to bother with JDBC access. To use them, you need to create a database object first. In our case, you will also need to copy the JDBC SQLite driver to the `lib` folder of your project directory like we did in the previous section. Note that, here and elsewhere when talking about SQL, we will concentrate on the basics rather than the elaborate details needed to develop enterprise-level applications. This is because for scientific purposes databases are usually used to store data and the issues of concurrency are usually not relevant:

```
import slick.driver.SQLiteDriver.api._
import scala.concurrent.ExecutionContext.Implicits.global
```

```
object SlickSQLite {
  def createPlanet: DBIO[Int] =
    sqlu"""CREATE TABLE planet(
    ID INT PRIMARY KEY NOT NULL,
    NAME TEXT NOT NULL,
    MASS REAL NOT NULL,
    PERIOD REAL NOT NULL)"""

  def main(args: Array[String]) {
    val db = Database.forURL("jdbc:sqlite:planets.sqlite",
    driver="org.sqlite.JDBC")
    try {
      db.run(createPlanet)
    } finally db.close()
  }
}
```

The preceding code will create the `planet` table we created in the previous section using low-level JDBC-based code. Here we create a `Database` object and then run an SQL query on it using the `run` method. The queries are built up via string interpolation using the `sql`, `sqlu`, and `tsql` interpolators. Interpolator `sql` is used for general queries that return a result set. Interpolator `sqlu` is used for update statements. The `tsql` interpolator is used to construct statements that can be type-checked during compile time.

If you want to insert the planet data in to the table, use the following function. Run it with `db.run` as before:

```
def populatePlanet: DBIO[Unit] = DBIO.seq(
  sqlu"""INSERT INTO planet
    VALUES (0, "Mercury", 3.3011E23, 0.240864)""",
  sqlu"""INSERT INTO planet
    VALUES (1, "Venus", 4.8675E24, 0.615)""",
  sqlu"""INSERT INTO planet
    VALUES (2, "Earth", 5.97237E24, 1)""",
  sqlu"""INSERT INTO planet
    VALUES (3, "Mars", 6.4171E23, 1.881)""",
  sqlu"""INSERT INTO planet
    VALUES (4, "Jupiter", 1.8986E27, 11.86)""",
  sqlu"""INSERT INTO planet
    VALUES (5, "Saturn", 5.6836E26, 29.46)""",
  sqlu"""INSERT INTO planet
    VALUES (6, "Uranus", 8.6810E25, 84.01)""",
  sqlu"""INSERT INTO planet
    VALUES (7, "Neptune", 1.0243E26, 164.8)"""
)
```

Reading and writing HDF5 files

Hierarchical Data Format (HDF) is a common file format for storing, organizing, and retrieving large amounts of data. It was developed by the National Center for Supercomputing Applications and remains a popular file format for storing large amounts of scientific data in a semi-structured format. The website of the group responsible for maintaining the HDF5 standard and the previous HDF4 standard, as well as the library for accessing these files and wrappers for many programming languages, is as follows: `https://www.hdfgroup.org/`.

Right now, there isn't a convenient way of accessing HDF5 files in a way that would use Scala's programming style and idioms. The reader is encouraged to use the Java libraries for HDF5 access instead. These libraries should be placed in the `lib` folder of your project and then can be used in much the same way they would be used in any Java program. To learn how to use the Java wrapper for the HDF5 libraries, consult the examples provided by the HDF group at the following address:

`https://www.hdfgroup.org/HDF5/examples/api18-java.html`

Summary

In this chapter, we looked in to data access in Scala. We considered reading and writing CSV, JSON, and XML files, as well as performing common database operations using SQL queries and Slick. We explored all of these using simple examples. The reader should be able to perform basic data storage and retrieval tasks in Scala now.

3
Numerical Computing with Breeze

Breeze is currently the most actively maintained and feature-rich numerical computing library available for Scala. It has data structures for vectors and matrices with real elements and efficient common matrix arithmetic operations. Breeze is similar in scope and purpose to MATLAB's data structures as well as the classes provided by the NumPy library for Python.

You can do basic matrix multiplication, inversion, dot products, determinants, and other operations expected from such a package. It also has a statistics package that contains common statistical distributions and other functions related to probability and statistics, such as Markov chain models. It includes several optimization algorithms. Functions useful for signal processing, such as Fourier transforms, convolution, and various filters are available.

It can also perform basic plotting. In this chapter, you will learn how to use this functionality to write programs for number crunching. Hopefully, by the end of it, you will be able to do most of the things you expect from a similar computing library on another platform. We will cover the following topics in this chapter:

- Using Breeze in your project
- Basic Breeze data structures
- Statistical computing with Breeze
- Optimization
- Signal processing
- Cheat sheet

Using Breeze in your project

Adding Breeze to your project is simple. As elsewhere in this book, we will be using SBT to handle our builds. Make a new directory for your project. Then, create a new file called `build.sbt` and add the following lines to it. You may want to change the versions to whatever the newest or preferred versions of Breeze and Scala are. Otherwise, you can probably just leave it as is:

```
libraryDependencies   ++= Seq(
  "org.scalanlp" %% "breeze" % "0.11.2",
  "org.scalanlp" %% "breeze-natives" % "0.11.2",
  "org.scalanlp" %% "breeze-viz" % "0.11.2"
)

scalaVersion := "2.11.5"
```

To play around with Breeze data structures, we will generally not want to create full programs using it. What we want is to just experiment a bit without committing to start a new project. It would be ideal if we could go into a Scala REPL to try the simple things with the Breeze libraries already loaded. Luckily, using SBT, this is easy to do. Once you create the `build.sbt` file provided here, issue the following `sbt` command from the terminal:

```
$ sbt console
```

After which, you will be dropped into the Scala REPL with the Breeze libraries loaded. And you didn't even need to create any source code files. All that is left is to import the relevant Breeze package and experiment.

Basic Breeze data structures

In this section, we will explore the basic data structures used to build Breeze programs. We will also discuss basic arithmetic operations that you can perform on these structures. The structures themselves are what you might expect from a numerical computing framework. If you have used MATLAB or Python's NumPy, you will instantly recognize them. The main ones you will probably be using are `DenseVector` and `DenseMatrix`. The sparse counterparts of these are `SparseVector` and `CSCMatrix`. These are optimized for use with large vectors and matrices that contain many zero elements. You can expect certain operations with these to be faster if your vectors and matrices fulfill the scarcity and largeness requirements. How sparse and large your data structures have to be for these to be worthwhile is not hard to guess. If you are dealing with sparse data structure, you should experiment and see if using `SparseVector` or `SparseMatrix` works faster.

DenseVector

Once in, the REPL lets us import the linear algebra routines:

```
scala> import breeze.linalg._
import breeze.linalg._
```

Creating `DenseVector` with user-defined elements is easy. You can just specify the values that the vector consists of in the constructor.

For example, the following code will construct a six-dimensional vector with values 1, 2, 3, 4, 5, and 6 at the corresponding coordinates. The type of the vector elements is then inferred from the arguments you used:

```
scala> val xs = DenseVector(1, 2, 3, 4, 5, 6)
xs: breeze.linalg.DenseVector[Int] = DenseVector(1, 2, 3, 4, 5, 6)
```

Alternatively, you can construct `DenseVector` using a Scala array:

```
scala> val arr: Array[Int] = Array(1, 2, 3, 4, 5, 6)
arr: Array[Int] = Array(1, 2, 3, 4, 5, 6)

scala> val xs = new DenseVector(arr)
xs: breeze.linalg.DenseVector[Int] = DenseVector(1, 2, 3, 4, 5, 6)
```

There is a further twist to the `DenseVector` data structure that is initialized from a Scala array, in that it does not have to contain all of the data contained in the array. You can also specify `offset` and `stride`. See the following example.

Here, we are taking every second element of the array. The ith element will then be calculated as *offset + i * stride*. An important point to consider here is that the `length` argument means the total number of elements in the constructed vector. If you miscalculate when using `stride`, `offset`, and `length`, you will run into exceptions:

```
scala> val xs = new DenseVector(arr, offset = 0, stride = 2, length = 3)
xs: breeze.linalg.DenseVector[Int] = DenseVector(1, 3, 5)
```

To get the length of a vector, use the `length` method:

```
scala> xs.length
res0: Int = 6
```

You can perform element-wise arithmetic operations on two vectors using the operators :+, :-, :*, and :/. These perform element-wise addition, subtraction, multiplication, and division, respectively. This is admittedly slightly less convenient than the corresponding operators in other systems. Let's create a new vector ys to illustrate:

```scala
scala> val ys = DenseVector(6, 5, 4, 3, 2, 1)
ys: breeze.linalg.DenseVector[Int] = DenseVector(6, 5, 4, 3, 2, 1)


scala> xs :+ ys
res0: breeze.linalg.DenseVector[Int] = DenseVector(7, 7, 7, 7, 7, 7)


scala> xs :- ys
res1: breeze.linalg.DenseVector[Int] = DenseVector(-5, -3, -1, 1, 3, 5)


scala> xs :* ys
res2: breeze.linalg.DenseVector[Int] = DenseVector(6, 10, 12, 12, 10, 6)


scala> xs :/ ys
res3: breeze.linalg.DenseVector[Int] = DenseVector(0, 0, 0, 1, 2, 6)
```

Multiplying by a scalar is always performed on all elements, as you would expect mathematically. The same is true of other operations with scalars as well as other mathematical functions:

```scala
scala> xs * 8
res8: breeze.linalg.DenseVector[Int] = DenseVector(8, 16, 24, 32, 40, 48)
```

You can use this fact to perform calculations on each element in a vector simultaneously. For example, we can translate the classic programming textbook example of Fahrenheit to Celsius conversion to vector notation. Here, we want to calculate the conversion for a number of values. We put these into a vector and then perform arithmetic operations with it as if it was a scalar variable.

First, we define two functions that operate on DenseVector. The first one takes a vector of values that represent temperature in degrees Fahrenheit and return a vector with corresponding temperatures in degrees Celsius:

```scala
scala> def f2c(fs: DenseVector[Double]): DenseVector[Double] = (fs - 32.0) / 1.8
f2c: (fs: breeze.linalg.DenseVector[Double])breeze.linalg.DenseVector[Double]
```

We then define a function that does the opposite. It takes a vector of values that represent temperatures in degrees Celsius and returns a vector with corresponding temperatures in degrees Fahrenheit:

```
scala> def c2f(cs: DenseVector[Double]): DenseVector[Double] = cs * 1.8 +
32.0

c2f: (cs: breeze.linalg.DenseVector[Double])breeze.linalg.
DenseVector[Double]
```

Now, let's test it out. We define a vector of values that represent temperature in degrees Celsius. These range from -20 to 40 degrees with a 10 degree increment. We can then use the functions we just defined to convert from degrees Celsius to degrees Fahrenheit and back. This is illustrated in the following code example:

```
scala> val cs = DenseVector(-20.0, -10.0, 0.0, 10.0, 20.0, 30.0, 40.0)

cs: breeze.linalg.DenseVector[Double] = DenseVector(-20.0, -10.0, 0.0,
10.0, 20.0, 30.0, 40.0)


scala> val fs = c2f(cs)

fs: breeze.linalg.DenseVector[Double] = DenseVector(-4.0, 14.0, 32.0,
50.0, 68.0, 86.0, 104.0)


scala> f2c(fs)

res0: breeze.linalg.DenseVector[Double] = DenseVector(-20.0, -10.0, 0.0,
10.0, 20.0, 30.0, 40.0)
```

A dot (or vector) product of two vectors is calculated by multiplying the elements of the vectors element-wise and then adding the resulting values together. This is equivalent to transposing one of the vectors and then performing matrix multiplication between them. Calculating a dot product of two vectors is simple in Breeze. Just use the dot method as shown in the following example:

```
scala> val xs = DenseVector(1.0, 2.0, 3.0, 4.0, 5.0)

xs: breeze.linalg.DenseVector[Double] = DenseVector(1.0, 2.0, 3.0, 4.0,
5.0)


scala> val ws = DenseVector(0.5, 1.0, 1.5, 2.0, 2.5)

ws: breeze.linalg.DenseVector[Double] = DenseVector(0.5, 1.0, 1.5, 2.0,
2.5)


scala> xs dot ws
res2: Double = 27.5
```

```
scala> xs dot ws
res3: Double = 27.5
```

Element-wise application of various standard mathematical functions is also easy. All you need to do is import `breeze.numerics._`. This will provide versions of functions in `scala.math` that will work on Breeze data structures. See the following simple example:

```
scala> import breeze.linalg._
import breeze.linalg._

scala> import breeze.numerics._
import breeze.numerics._

scala> import scala.math.Pi
import scala.math.Pi

scala> val x = DenseVector(0.0, 0.5 * Pi, Pi, 1.5 * Pi, 2.0 * Pi)
x: breeze.linalg.DenseVector[Double] = DenseVector(0.0,
1.5707963267948966, 3.141592653589793, 4.71238898038469,
6.283185307179586)

scala> sin(x)
res2: breeze.linalg.DenseVector[Double] = DenseVector(0.0, 1.0,
1.2246467991473532E-16, -1.0, -2.4492935982947064E-16)

scala> cos(x)
res3: breeze.linalg.DenseVector[Double] = DenseVector(1.0,
6.123233995736766E-17, -1.0, -1.8369701987210297E-16, 1.0)
```

 For the other mathematical functions available, look at the documentation of the numerics package:
http://www.scalanlp.org/api/breeze/index.html#breeze.numerics.package

Finally, to illustrate some of the concepts outlined here, look at the following function that calculates the Euclidean distance between two vectors:

```
def distance(v1: DenseVector[Double], v2: DenseVector[Double]):
Double = {
    val diff = v1 :- v2
    diff dot diff
}
```

DenseMatrix

DenseMatrix is probably the data structure you will use most in Breeze for most numerical problems. There are several ways to create matrices. A lot of the following will also work with DenseVector.

If you want to create a matrix filled with user-specified values directly, you can do it in a way similar to the one used with vectors. You just need to separate the rows of the matrix with parentheses:

```scala
scala> val x = DenseMatrix((1.0, 3.0, 5.0), (2.0, 4.0, 6.0))
x: breeze.linalg.DenseMatrix[Double] =
1.0   3.0   5.0
2.0   4.0   6.0
```

You can create a matrix from an array similar to how you did with DenseVector. However, in this case, you will also have to specify the shape of the matrix as well:

```scala
scala> val x = new DenseMatrix(2, 3, Array(1.0, 2.0, 3.0, 4.0, 5.0, 6.0))
x: breeze.linalg.DenseMatrix[Double] =
1.0   3.0   5.0
2.0   4.0   6.0
```

Obviously, the array you use will have to contain the number of elements equal to rows times columns specified. The first number in the constructor specifies the number of rows and the second one specifies the number of columns.

You can also create a matrix filled with a specified value. Commonly, this value is zero. To create a zero-filled matrix, you can use the zeros method as shown here:

```scala
scala> val x = DenseMatrix.zeros[Double](2, 3)
x: breeze.linalg.DenseMatrix[Double] =
0.0   0.0   0.0
0.0   0.0   0.0
```

To get a matrix filled with ones, you can use the ones method as illustrated by the following:

```scala
scala> val x = DenseMatrix.ones[Double](2, 3)
x: breeze.linalg.DenseMatrix[Double] =
1.0   1.0   1.0
1.0   1.0   1.0
```

You can also create a matrix filled with any value as follows:

```scala
scala> val x = DenseMatrix.fill(2, 3){4.0}
x: breeze.linalg.DenseMatrix[Double] =
4.0   4.0   4.0
4.0   4.0   4.0
```

It's also possible to create an identity matrix:

```scala
scala> val x = DenseMatrix.eye[Double](3)
x: breeze.linalg.DenseMatrix[Double] =
1.0   0.0   0.0
0.0   1.0   0.0
0.0   0.0   1.0
```

It is also possible to create a matrix from a function. This is nice when you want to initialize a matrix or vector with useful values. If constructing vectors, the function has to take a single argument, which is the index of the element vector. The function you use for matrices will have to take two arguments, those being the row and column of the element. This allows for easy creation of matrices from data, for example. Alternatively, you may want to fill a matrix with precalculated data using a mathematical function like sine, cosine, and many more:

```scala
scala> val v = DenseVector.tabulate(5){i => sin(2.0 * Pi * (i / 5.0))}
v: breeze.linalg.DenseVector[Double] = DenseVector(0.0,
0.9510565162951535, 0.5877852522924732, -0.587785252292473,
-0.9510565162951536)


scala> val x = DenseMatrix.tabulate(2, 3){case (i, j) => i + j}
x: breeze.linalg.DenseMatrix[Int] =
0   1   2
1   2   3
```

You can then use matrix operations on the DenseMatrix objects. They work the way that you would expect from linear algebra. Important operations include matrix multiplication, linear solve, determinant, inverse, and others. For example, to calculate a matrix product, you can simply use the multiplication operator * as shown here:

```scala
scala> val A = DenseMatrix((3, 2, 5), (8, -3, 3))
A: breeze.linalg.DenseMatrix[Int] =
3   2   5
```

```
8   -3   3
```

```
scala> val B = DenseMatrix((8, -4), (0, 7), (1, -5))
B: breeze.linalg.DenseMatrix[Int] =
8   -4
0   7
1   -5
```

```
scala> val result = A * B
result: breeze.linalg.DenseMatrix[Int] =
29   -23
67   -68
```

To linearly solve a system of equations $A x = B$ for x, you can use the backslash (rather than the division operator). The result in the last evaluation is not mathematically correct due to the floating point rounding errors:

```
scala> val A = DenseMatrix((1.0, 2.0, 3.0), (4.0, 5.0, 6.0))
A: breeze.linalg.DenseMatrix[Double] =
1.0   2.0   3.0
4.0   5.0   6.0
```

```
scala> val B = DenseMatrix((7.0), (8.0))
B: breeze.linalg.DenseMatrix[Double] =
7.0
8.0
```

```
scala> val x = A \ B
x: breeze.linalg.DenseMatrix[Double] =
-3.0555555555555554
0.11111111111111155
3.27777777777777
```

```
scala> A * x
res0: breeze.linalg.DenseMatrix[Double] =
6.999999999999998
7.999999999999964
```

To calculate the inverse of a matrix, you can use the `inv` function. The results of rounding errors are again apparent:

```
scala> val A = DenseMatrix((1.0, 2.0), (3.0, 4.0))
A: breeze.linalg.DenseMatrix[Double] =
1.0   2.0
3.0   4.0

scala> val invA = inv(A)
invA: breeze.linalg.DenseMatrix[Double] =
-1.999999999999996    0.9999999999999998
1.499999999999998    -0.4999999999999999

scala> A * invA
res20: breeze.linalg.DenseMatrix[Double] =
1.0                    0.0
8.881784197001252E-16  0.9999999999999996
```

To calculate the determinant of a matrix, you can use the `det` function:

```
scala> det(A)
res0: Double = -2.0
```

Indexing and slicing

We will use indexing and slicing to select elements from matrices and to create new matrices containing a subset of the original matrix. In the simplest case, you can just specify the row and column of the matrix element you want, as demonstrated here:

```
scala> val x = DenseMatrix((1, 2, 3), (4, 5, 6))
x: breeze.linalg.DenseMatrix[Int] =
1  2  3
4  5  6

scala> val y = x(1, 2)
y: Int = 6
```

You can select a subset of a vector using the familiar range notation. Both `to` and `until` versions will work as you might expect:

```scala
scala> val vx = DenseVector(1, 2, 3, 4, 5, 6)
vx: breeze.linalg.DenseVector[Int] = DenseVector(1, 2, 3, 4, 5, 6)


scala> val vy = vx(1 to 3)
vy: breeze.linalg.DenseVector[Int] = DenseVector(2, 3, 4)


scala> val vy = vx(1 until 3)
vy: breeze.linalg.DenseVector[Int] = DenseVector(2, 3)
```

To select a row of a matrix, you can do the following:

```scala
scala> val y = x(1, ::)
y: breeze.linalg.Transpose[breeze.linalg.DenseVector[Int]] =
Transpose(DenseVector(4, 5, 6))
```

Similarly, you can also select a column:

```scala
scala> val y = x(::, 1)
y: breeze.linalg.DenseVector[Int] = DenseVector(2, 5)
```

You can use negative numbers as indices to select elements starting from the end. For example, to select the last element, just use minus one. To select the next to last element use minus two and so on:

```scala
scala> val last = y(-1)
last: Int = 5
```

Reshaping

The shape of a matrix refers to the number of rows and columns in that matrix. To get the shape of a matrix, you can request the number of rows and columns separately as shown here:

```scala
scala> val x = DenseMatrix((1, 2, 3), (4, 5, 6))
x: breeze.linalg.DenseMatrix[Int] =
1  2  3
4  5  6


scala> val rows = x.rows
```

```
rows: Int = 2
```

```
scala> val cols = x.cols
cols: Int = 3
```

Reshaping a matrix refers to changing its number of rows and/or columns while at the same time retaining the same data in some sense. Transposing a vector can be seen as a kind of reshaping, although in Breeze, the transpose method on a vector will not result in the shape being changed. An example of reshaping a matrix by switching its rows and columns is given here. Reshaping will be a familiar operation to users of other numerical computing libraries. For example, to convert a matrix into a vector with the same elements, you can use the following commands:

```
scala> val x = DenseMatrix((1, 2, 3), (4, 5, 6))
x: breeze.linalg.DenseMatrix[Int] =
1  2  3
4  5  6
```

```
scala> val y = x.reshape(1, 6)
y: breeze.linalg.DenseMatrix[Int] = 1  4  2  5  3  6
```

To flatten a matrix, you can also use the toDenseVector method as shown in the following example. For this example, the result will be the same:

```
scala> x.toDenseVector
res0: breeze.linalg.DenseVector[Int] = DenseVector(1, 4, 2, 5, 3, 6)
```

Concatenation

The act of concatenation is used to join two vectors or matrices in some way. For vectors, it can simply be "attaching" one vector to the end of another. Alternatively, you may want those two vectors to become the columns of a matrix, and so on.

To concatenate two vectors to form a longer vector, you can use the vertcat method provided by the DenseVector class:

```
scala> val v1 = DenseVector(1, 2, 3)
v1: breeze.linalg.DenseVector[Int] = DenseVector(1, 2, 3)
```

```
scala> val v2 = DenseVector(4, 5, 6)
v2: breeze.linalg.DenseVector[Int] = DenseVector(4, 5, 6)
```

```
scala> DenseVector.vertcat(v1, v2)
res0: breeze.linalg.DenseVector[Int] = DenseVector(1, 2, 3, 4, 5, 6)
```

When concatenating matrices, the principle is basically the same as when concatenating vectors. However, now you can concatenate both vertically and horizontally. Obviously, the shape of the matrices has to be compatible. When concatenating vertically, they have to have the same number of columns, and when concatenating horizontally, they have to have the same number of rows. Matrix concatenation is illustrated by the following examples:

```
scala> val m1 = DenseMatrix((1, 2, 3))
m1: breeze.linalg.DenseMatrix[Int] = 1  2  3


scala> val m2 = DenseMatrix((4, 5, 6))
m2: breeze.linalg.DenseMatrix[Int] = 4  5  6


scala> DenseMatrix.vertcat(m1, m2)
res0: breeze.linalg.DenseMatrix[Int] =
1  2  3
4  5  6


scala> DenseMatrix.horzcat(m1.t, m2.t)
res1: breeze.linalg.DenseMatrix[Int] =
1  4
2  5
3  6
```

In the first example, we concatenate two matrices vertically. This means they are stacked on top of each other. In the second example, we concatenate horizontally. We transpose the matrices first, because otherwise they will be appended end to end just like in the `DenseVector` example.

Statistical computing with Breeze

Generating vectors and matrices of random values from a specified distribution is a very common task in most kinds of simulation software. The statistics-related stuff in Breeze is kept in the `breeze.stats.distributions` package. Before doing anything, we will need to import it:

```
scala> import breeze.stats.distributions._
import breeze.stats.distributions._
```

Now, to fill a vector with uniformly distributed values in the interval *[0, 1]*, you can use the `Uniform` distribution:

```scala
scala> val u = Uniform(0.0, 1.0)
u: breeze.stats.distributions.Uniform = Uniform(0.0,1.0)
```

To draw a sample from a distribution, you use the `sample` method. You can specify the number of samples to draw. In which case, a vector will be returned:

```scala
scala> val sample = u.sample(5)
sample: IndexedSeq[Double] = Vector(0.314402432799765,
0.9148520439005925, 0.8929580216449953, 0.9447241194598741,
0.5203139296795614)


scala> val rv = DenseVector(sample)
rv: breeze.linalg.DenseVector[IndexedSeq[Double]] = DenseVector(V
ector(0.314402432799765, 0.9148520439005925, 0.8929580216449953,
0.9447241194598741, 0.5203139296795614))
```

You can create a matrix filled with random values similarly. However, in this case, you will also need to specify the shape of the matrix. See an example of how this can be done:

```scala
scala> val x = new DenseMatrix(5, 3, u.sample(15).toArray)
x: breeze.linalg.DenseMatrix[Double] =
0.7185216398668066    0.826088764652877     0.08671888826547725
0.6028323551929327    0.15966791379084433   0.3516343444499279
0.02433037735002519   0.3549970097752144    0.42881957314072827
0.6954470616231088    0.618911119884477     0.2831518443130081
0.9469487268548222    0.34730749385171067   0.45877989424568866
```

To get a single sample out of a distribution, you can use the `draw` method:

```scala
scala> u.draw
res0: Double = 0.2010005823693246
```

Here, we present a table with other distributions and their parameters. All these distributions can be used to draw samples from in the same way as we did with the preceding uniform distribution. The parameters are the arguments to the constructor. For any of these distributions, you instantiate it as shown here for the Beta distribution. Here, 5.0 and 1.0 are the values of the arguments *a* and *b*:

```scala
val beta = new Beta(5.0, 1.0)
```

Distribution	Parameter 1	Parameter 2	Description
Uniform	`Low: Double`	`High: Double`	Draw uniformly distributed samples between the `High` and `Low` values.
Beta	`a: Double`	`b: Double`	Draw samples from the `Beta` distribution over *[0, 1]*. Parameters *a* and *b* stand for alpha and beta parameters, respectively.
Binomial	`n: Int`	`p: Double`	Draw samples from the binomial distribution where *n* samples are drawn with probability of success *p*.
ChiSquared	`k: Double`	`n/a`	Draw samples from the chi-squared distribution with *k* degrees of freedom.
Dirichlet	`space: TensorSpace`	`n/a`	Draw samples from the Dirichlet distribution. Argument `space` has to be a *k*-dimensional vector if you need *k*-dimensional samples. The values in vector `space` will then be Dirichlet distribution parameters.
Exponential	`rate: Double`	`n/a`	Draw samples from the exponential distribution with the rate (or lambda) parameter.
Gamma	`shape: Double`	`scale: Double`	Draw samples from the gamma distribution with a given shape and scale parameters.
Gaussian	`mu: Double`	`sigma: Double`	Draw from the Gaussian distribution with mean *mu* and standard deviation *sigma*.

Distribution	Parameter 1	Parameter 2	Description
Geometric	p: Double	n/a	Draw numbers from the geometric distribution. It calculates the probability for the number of trials until the first success where each trial has the probability of success *p*.
LogNormal	mu: Double	sigma: Double	Draw samples from log-normal distribution with mean *mu* and standard deviation *sigma*.
NegativeBinomial	r: Double	p: Double	Draw from the negative binomial distribution. The number of failures is *r* and the probability of success is *p*.
Poisson	mean: Double	n/a	Draw from the Poisson distribution with a user-specified expected value.
Polya	space: TensorSpace	n/a	Draw from the Polya distribution. Here, parameter space can be a vector with distribution parameters.
VonMises	mu: Double	k: Double	Draw from the von Mises distribution with mode *mu* and dispersion *k*.

To calculate the mean, variance, standard deviation, and other simple descriptive statistics for a data vector, you can use the functions `mean`, `variance`, `stddev`, and `meanAndVariance`. These work as you might expect them to. The `meanAndVariance` function will return the mean, variance, and number of elements in the vector. You need to import them from the `breeze.stats` package. An example of their use is given here:

```scala
scala> import breeze.linalg._
import breeze.linalg._
```

```
scala> import breeze.stats._
import breeze.stats._

scala> import breeze.stats.distributions._
import breeze.stats.distributions._

scala> val u = Uniform(0.8, 2.3)
u: breeze.stats.distributions.Uniform = Uniform(0.8,2.3)

scala> val v = new DenseVector(u.sample(10).toArray)
v: breeze.linalg.DenseVector[Double] = DenseVector(2.0363433987517316,
0.92140150463495, 0.9528215299165498, 1.7466840166261823,
1.6714672536703268, 1.0814385804087956, 1.3805359690241807,
1.0814690985863498, 1.8617474004800583, 1.9304861680381757)

scala> mean(v)
res0: Double = 1.46643949201373

scala> variance(v)
res1: Double = 0.18684984880609112

scala> stddev(v)
res2: Double = 0.4322613004389556

scala> meanAndVariance(v)
res3: breeze.stats.MeanAndVariance =
MeanAndVariance(1.464394920137303,0.18684984880609112,10)
```

Optimization

Optimization deals with finding the minimum value of a function. In the case of real-valued function optimization, the function maps vectors of real values to real values. The argument of the function usually represents a solution to a real-life problem. The result of the function is usually the evaluation of that solution, that is, a numerical estimate of how well the solution in question solves the problem. The global minimum is defined as the function argument (a vector) that gives the lowest (or highest) function value. That is, there has to be no other argument vector that would result in a function value that is lower or higher.

Most often, optimization methods do not guarantee finding the global minimum, and you have to settle for a local minimum. A local minimum is the solution that minimizes the function within some local area of the function surface (although don't quote that definition anywhere). You can look up more information about optimization in literature that is specific to optimization. One group of popular optimization methods are gradient-descent methods that require the function to be once or twice differentiable and use that information to find local minima. We will examine the tools for optimization supplied by Breeze. For most of these, you will need to create an instance of `DiffFunction`, which will return both a functions value and its first order gradient at a given solution. Let's consider a very simple function that consists of a parabola with its center (and thus global minimum) at the solution *(-1, 2, -4)*. A parabola was chosen because we can guarantee that the gradient-descent optimization methods will find the global minimum and because the derivatives are very easy to calculate:

```scala
import breeze.linalg._
import scala.math.{pow}
import breeze.optimize._

object Optimization {
  val fn = new DiffFunction[DenseVector[Double]] {
    def calculate(x: DenseVector[Double]) = {
      (pow(x(0) + 1.0, 2.0) +
       pow(x(1) - 2.0, 2.0) +
       pow(x(2) + 4.0, 2.0),
       DenseVector(2.0 * (x(0) + 1),
         2.0 * (x(1) - 2.0),
         2.0 * (x(2) + 4.0)))
    }
  }

  def main(args: Array[String]) {
    val minimum = DenseVector(-1.0, 2.0, -4.0)
    println(fn.valueAt(minimum))
    println(fn.gradientAt(minimum))
    println(fn.calculate(minimum))
  }
}
```

The preceding program should output the following lines to the console when run with `sbt run`:

```
0.0
DenseVector(0.0, 0.0, 0.0)
(0.0,DenseVector(0.0, 0.0, 0.0))
```

Alternatively, if you cannot be bothered to calculate the derivative of your function, you can approximate it using the provided `ApproximateGradientFunction` class. This will give a numerical approximation of the derivative at any given point. For this to work well, your function has to be easy to compute, because approximating a gradient numerically will require several evaluations of the function:

```scala
scala> def fn(x: DenseVector[Double]) = pow(x(0) + 1.0, 2.0) + pow(x(1) -
2.0, 2.0) + pow(x(2) + 4.0, 2.0)
fn: (x: breeze.linalg.DenseVector[Double])Double

scala> val diffFn = new ApproximateGradientFunction(fn)
diffFn: breeze.optimize.ApproximateGradientFunction[Int,breeze.linalg.
DenseVector[Double]] = <function1>
scala> diffFn.gradientAt(DenseVector(-1.0, 2.0, -4.0))
res0: breeze.linalg.DenseVector[Double] = DenseVector(9.99999999990897
9E-6, 1.0000000000131023E-5, 1.0000000000131023E-5)
```

Now that we have our function, we can use the provided optimization functions. For example, we could use the `LBFGS` function, which implements the Broyden–Fletcher–Goldfarb–Shanno method. An example that minimizes the function we defined is given here:

```scala
def main(args: Array[String]) {
  val lbfgs = new LBFGS[DenseVector[Double]](maxIter=100,
    m=10, tolerance=0.001)
  val solution = lbfgs.minimize(fn, DenseVector(0.0, 0.0, 0.0))
  println(solution)
}
```

Here, we redefine the main method of our previous program. The meaning of the arguments to the `LBFGS` function is as follows: `maxIter` — the maximum number of iterations that the algorithm will do; `m` — a parameter that influences memory consumption (seek out information about the method to understand its exact meaning, otherwise you can leave it as default 10); and `tolerance` — convergence tolerance. The `minimize` method then takes the function as a starting point. If you don't know much about the function, you can use a random value within the feasible region. The **feasible region** is basically the region in the solution space where the value of your function is not undefined. We used a zero vector here. The method has no problems finding the minimum value in this case, as is evident from the following result. The values are, of course, approximate. You can increase accuracy by lowering the tolerance and increasing the maximum number of iterations. If you want to guarantee that the method finds the local minimum to within a given precision, you will need to set the maximum iterations parameter fairly high:

```
DenseVector(-1.000000000000002, 2.0000000000000004,
-4.000000000000001)
```

You can find other optimization methods in the `breeze.optimize` package. Most of them work in the same or a similar way to the method we examined above. You have to supply `DiffFunction` and then maybe provide method-specific parameters. A full list of the methods that are available can be found in the API documentation of the package.

`http://www.scalanlp.org/api/breeze/index.html#breeze.optimize.package`

Signal processing

Breeze has several methods to help you write digital signal processing code. These include functions for convolution, Fourier transforms, and several digital filters. These are useful when you are dealing with digital signals, such as sound and others. Anyone working with sound, speech, image processing, and other similar areas, such as pattern recognition, will find these useful. In this section, we will also use Breeze's plotting facilities to help us illustrate some concepts.

Fourier transforms

Fourier transforms are named after Joseph Fourier, who, in 1822, showed that some functions can be written as the (possibly) infinite sum of harmonics. Getting into the topic of Fourier analysis is out of the scope of this book. It will be assumed that the reader knows what they are and what they are useful for. We will simply show you how to do discrete Fourier transforms using Breeze. Here, we present a program that does a Fourier transform on a simple signal that consists of the sum of several sinusoids. In this case, we expect the transform to show peaks at the frequencies of those sinusoids:

```
import breeze.linalg._
import scala.math.{sin, Pi}
import breeze.signal._
import breeze.plot._

object FFTDemo {
  def calculateSignal(index: Int, size: Int): Double = {
    val fIndex = index.toDouble
    val fSize = size.toDouble
    (0.1 * sin(fIndex / fSize * 5.0 * 2.0 * Pi) +
     0.4 * sin(fIndex / fSize * 10.0 * 2.0 * Pi) +
     0.5 * sin(fIndex / fSize * 50.0 * 2.0 * Pi))
  }
```

```scala
def main(args: Array[String]) {
  val signal = DenseVector.tabulate(512){i => calculateSignal(i,
                                                                512)}
  val f = Figure()
  val p = f.subplot(0)
  val x = linspace(0.0, 512.0, 512)
  p += plot(x, signal)
  p.xlabel = "sample"
  p.ylabel = "value"
  f.saveas("signal.png")
}
}
```

First, we import the relevant packages. This also includes `breeze.plot`, which contains Breeze's (still somewhat basic) plotting routines. The actual meat of the program consists of adding three sinusoids with different frequencies and amplitudes. This is done in the `calculateSignal` function. This function is then used to fill in a 512-element `DenseVector` with samples that represent our signal. The signal is then plotted and saved to a file called `signal.png`. You can see the results of running the program in the following figure:

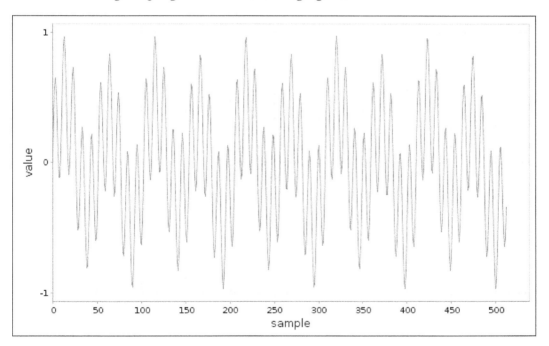

We will now, as per the topic at hand, perform Fourier analysis on our signal. This can be done using the `fourierTransform` function that can take a `DenseVector` of complex numbers. To plot the Fourier transformation of the signal, we have to rewrite the `main` method as follows:

```
def main(args: Array[String]) {
  val signal = DenseVector.tabulate(512){i => calculateSignal(i,
                                                               512)}
  val f = Figure()
  val p = f.subplot(0)
  val x = linspace(0.0, 256.0, 256)
  val csignal = for (sample <- signal)
    yield new Complex(sample, 0.0)
  val transformed = fourierTransform(csignal)
  val amplitudes = for (bin <- transformed)
    yield bin.abs
  val firstHalf = amplitudes(0 until 256)
  p += plot(x, firstHalf)
  p.xlabel = "bin"
  p.ylabel = "amplitude"
  f.saveas("transformed.png")
}
```

The result of running the program is shown in *Figure 2*. The peaks represent our sinusoids. As you can see, they appear at the 5th, 10th, and 50th bins in the plot. This corresponds to the multipliers we used when calculating the signal. The height of the peaks is in line with their relative amplitudes.

Inverse Fourier transforms are easy as well. Use the `inverseFourierTransform` function. For example, the following code will calculate the Fourier transform of the signal and then convert it back to time domain with `inverseFourierTransform`. You can transform the frequency domain representation of the signal as you see fit between the two transformations:

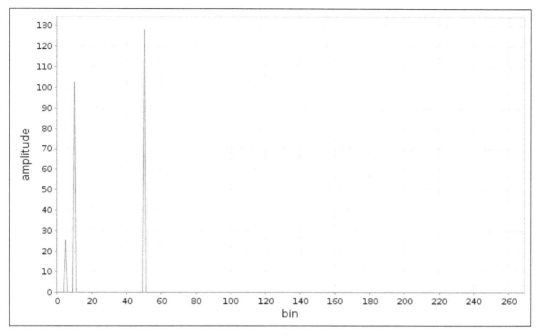

Figure 2

```
val transformed = fourierTransform(signal)
// Manipulate the frequency domain representation here.
val reconstructed = inverseFourierTransform(transformed)
```

Other signal processing functionality

Other signal processing functionality (what little there currently is in Breeze) can be found in the `breeze.signal` package. The `convolve` and `correlate` functions that perform discrete convolution and correlation over two vectors, respectively, may be of interest to people. The reader is encouraged to take a look at the Breeze API documentation for the `breeze.signal` package, which can be found at the following link:

`http://www.scalanlp.org/api/breeze/index.html#breeze.signal.package`

Cheat sheet

In the following tables, we summarize the concepts presented in this chapter. In addition, we also provide examples of how the same things are accomplished in NumPy and MATLAB. Use this to quickly look up common idioms when you are starting out with Breeze. Note that this only includes basic operations. We do not cover more advanced topics such as optimization and signal processing.

Creating matrices and vectors

Here, we examine the various ways of creating vectors and matrices in the three different systems:

Operation	Breeze	NumPy	MATLAB
Matrix creation (inline)	`DenseMatrix((1.0, 2.0), (3.0, 4.0))`	`np.array([[1.0, 2.0], [3.0, 4.0]])`	`[1 2; 3 4]`
Vector creation (inline)	`DenseVector(1.0, 2.0, 3.0, 4.0)`	`np.array([1.0, 2.0, 3.0, 4.0])`	`[1 2 3 4]`
Transpose	`vector.t`	`array.transpose()`	`vector'`
Zero matrix	`DenseMatrix.zeros[Double](n, m)`	`np.zeros((n, m))`	`zeros(n, m)`
Zero vector	`DenseVector.zeros[Double](n)`	`np.zeros(n)`	`zeros(n)`
Matrix filled with a given number	`DenseMatrix.fill(n, m){nr}`	`array.fill(nr)`	`ones(n, m) * nr`
Vector filled with a given number	`DenseVector.fill(n){nr}`	`array.fill(nr)`	`ones(1, n) * nr`
Matrix filled with random numbers in the interval (0, 1)	`DenseMatrix.rand(n, m)`	`np.random.random((n, m))`	`rand(n, m)`
Vector filled with random numbers in the interval (0, 1)	`DenseVector.rand(n)`	`np.random.random(n)`	`rand(1, n)`

Operations on matrices and vectors

In the following table, we summarize the types of operations on matrices and vectors that were discussed in this chapter as well as how you would do the same things in NumPy and MATLAB:

Operation	Breeze	NumPy	MATLAB
Element-wise addition	`v1 :+ v2`	`v1 + v2`	`v1 + v2`
Element-wise subtraction	`v1 :- v2`	`v1 - v2`	`v1 - v2`
Element-wise multiplication	`v1 :* v2`	`v1 * v2`	`v1 .* v2`
Element-wise division	`v1 :/ v2`	`v1 / v2`	`v1 ./ v2`
Dot product	`v1 dot v2`	`np.dot(v1, v2)`	`dot(v1, v2)`
Linear solve	`v1 / v2`	`v1 / v2`	`np.linalg.solve(v1, v2)`

Summary

In this chapter, we examined how to use the Breeze numerical computing library for common linear algebra, optimizations, and signal processing tasks. The basic operations with Breeze's vector and matrix types were described. We have seen how to add, multiply, subtract, and divide matrices and vectors element wise. You also learned how to apply mathematical functions to them element wise.

We have also seen how to create new matrices and vectors initialized with various initial data, Breeze's statistical distributions, and drawing samples from them. The optimization functionality available in Breeze was briefly described. We have seen how to optimize a simple function using the LBFGS optimization method. We have seen how to perform Fourier analysis on signals as well as how to plot the results of said analysis.

Upon reading this chapter, you should have a good idea how to perform common numerical computing tasks. Operations available in other numerical computing platforms such as NumPy and MATLAB are available in Breeze as well. We have tried to show you how to best use them to achieve your goals.

4
Using Saddle for Data Analysis

Saddle is a library for manipulating structured data. It is written in Scala and the authors claim that it is "the easiest and most expressive way to program with structured data on the JVM." It draws inspiration from and replicates a lot of the functionality of **R** and **pandas** Python library. It also occupies a similar niche in scientific computing as those two systems. In addition, it provides access to similar data structures to NumPy and Breeze (to represent matrices and vectors), that is you can use it to write numerical computing code as well.

While it can be used for various things, it is mostly used for data analysis, namely, for analyzing data arranged into a two-dimensional table with named columns and indexed rows. This type of structured data is probably familiar to you if you have ever done any kind of work in pattern recognition, data mining, and many other disciplines. Or, for that matter, if you have ever used spreadsheet software or SQL databases. This data can then be analyzed using various descriptive statistics, plotted, filtered, grouped, and much more.

You can also use the data structures supplied to implement various more involved data analysis or visualization methods. How all of this can be done will be seen in this chapter. But first, we will discuss the data structures and basic functionality it provides.

- Installing Saddle
- Basic Saddle data structures
- Data analysis with Saddle

Installing Saddle

The website for Saddle is as follows:

`https://saddle.github.io/`

Before beginning to delve into the functionality provided by the library, we want to make the Saddle library available to your project. As in previous instances, we will use SBT to handle dependencies and build our project. Start a new directory for this chapter (call it `saddle` or something more creative if you like). You will need to create a new `build.sbt` file and put the following directives in it:

```
resolvers ++= Seq(
  "Sonatype Snapshots" at
  "http://oss.sonatype.org/content/repositories/snapshots",
  "Sonatype Releases" at
  "http://oss.sonatype.org/content/repositories/releases"
)

libraryDependencies ++= Seq(
  "org.scala-saddle" %% "saddle-core" % "1.3.+"
)

scalaVersion := "2.11.6"
```

Alternatively, you can set different versions for Saddle and Scala by modifying the version numbers in this file. After you create the file, you can go into the REPL with the Saddle library available for import by running the `sbt console` command from the directory where the `build.sbt` file is.

Basic Saddle data structures

In this section, we will examine the basic data structures available to you when using Saddle. A lot of these you will recognize from similar data types in other systems. We will generally only quickly overview them. More advanced uses are covered in other sections. All of the examples in this section can be done from the REPL. We will only need to start creating separate `.scala` files when we come to the more elaborate examples in the other sections. To start working with any of the following code examples, you need to first import the Saddle package:

```
scala> import org.saddle._
import org.saddle._
```

Using the Vec structure

The simplest type covered here is the vector. It is closest to a simple array in terms of functionality. On top of the functions expected from a one-dimensional array kind-of-type, there are also various mathematical functions defined for them. Let's see what those are. First of all, you will want to create a vector. The simplest way to create a vector is to specify the values that you want it to be filled with:

```scala
scala> Vec(1, 2, 3, 4, 5, 6)
res0: org.saddle.Vec[Int] =
[6 x 1]
1
2
3
4
5
6
```

Alternatively, you may want to create a vector from a Scala array. You can do it as shown here (since the string representation of Saddle objects can be large, we will omit the REPL output sometimes):

```scala
scala> Vec(Array(1, 2, 3, 4, 5, 6))
```

You can also initialize a vector filled with ones, zeros, and random values:

```scala
scala> vec.ones(10)
scala> vec.zeros(10)
scala> vec.rand(10)
scala> vec.randn(10)
scala> vec.randn2(10, -1.0, 2.0)
```

The last three examples will create vectors with 10 random values from the range -1.0 to 1.0, 10 random values from the normal distribution with mean 0.0 and standard deviation 1.0, and 10 random values with mean -1.0 and standard deviation 2.0, respectively.

Using arithmetic operations in Vec

All the arithmetic operations are defined for vectors, and they operate element-wise. See an example here:

```
scala> val v1 = Vec(1, 2, 3)
v1: org.saddle.Vec[Int] =
[3 x 1]
1
2
3

scala> val v2 = Vec(4, 5, 6)
v2: org.saddle.Vec[Int] =
[3 x 1]
4
5
6

scala> v1 + v2
res12: org.saddle.Vec[Int] =
[3 x 1]
5
7
9
```

The preceding example adds the vectors element-wise and creates a new vector containing the sums of elements of the two vectors as its elements.

Other operations on vectors are given here. Here, the ** operator raises the elements of the first vector to the power given by the elements of the other vector (element wise):

```
scala> v1 - v2
scala> v1 * v2
scala> v1 / v2
scala> v1 ** v2
```

Also, `dot` and `outer` products are defined. If the vectors are column vectors (and they are in Saddle), the result of the `dot` product is the same as if you transposed the first vector (the operand on the left) and then multiplied them using matrix multiplication. The result is a single number. The result of the `outer` product is the same as transposing the second vector and using matrix multiplication. This results in a matrix:

```
scala> v1 dot v2
res0: Int = 32


scala> v1 outer v2
res1: org.saddle.Mat[Int] =
[3 x 3]
  4   5   6
  8  10  12
 12  15  18
```

Also, operations with scalars are defined. However, the scalar has to be the right operand. This is a Scala quirk and has to do with the fact that all binary operators are simply methods with the element on the right being the argument for the method:

```
scala> v1 + 2.0
scala> v1 - 2.0
scala> v1 * 2.0
scala> v1 / 2.0
scala> v1 ** 2.0
```

Data access in Vec

Now, let's move on to accessing data stored in vectors. A lot of these functions will be familiar to you from other similar systems as well as from Breeze, which was discussed in the previous chapter:

```
scala> val v = Vec(1, 1, 2, 3, 5, 8)
```

You can then access elements of the vector using the `at()` method:

```
scala> v.at(2)
res0: org.saddle.scalar.Scalar[Int] = 2
```

You can also access multiple elements of the vector. Simply write the indices of the elements you want and a new vector will be formed with elements at those indices:

```scala
scala> v(1, 3, 5)
res0: org.saddle.Vec[Int] =
[3 x 1]
1
3
8
```

The following three examples show how to get part of a vector conveniently using the range notation. The first example will return a three-element vector containing elements 1, 2, and 3 of vector v. The second example will return the first three elements, while the last example will return all elements starting with the element with index 2 to the end of the vector:

```scala
scala> v(1 -> 3)
scala> v(* -> 2)
scala> v(2 -> *)
```

Implementing the slice method in Vec

You can also use the `slice()` method to select part of a vector. See the following examples. The first example should be self-explanatory. The second example uses the third parameter to skip every second element:

```scala
scala> v.slice(1, 3)
res0: org.saddle.Vec[Int] =
[2 x 1]
1
2

scala> v.slice(0, 5, 2)
res1: org.saddle.Vec[Int] =
[3 x 1]
1
2
5
```

Statistic calculation in Vec

Finally, you can also calculate some descriptive statistics for values stored in vectors. Some of the methods to do so are given here. The first two examples show how to calculate the sum and product of the elements contained in the vector. The purpose of the other methods should be apparent from their names:

```scala
scala> val v = vec.randn2(10, -2.0, 0.1)


scala> v.sum
res0: Double = -20.68555444404416


scala> v.prod
res1: Double = 1412.0730387240915
scala> v.mean
res2: Double = -2.0685554444044163


scala> v.median
res3: Double = -2.0673818292154023


scala> v.min
res4: Option[Double] = Some(-2.281467544572)


scala> v.max
res5: Option[Double] = Some(-1.7973015168985262)


scala> v.stdev
res6: Double = 0.12029393523525414


scala> v.variance
res7: Double = 0.014470630854383519
```

Using the Mat structure

Mat is the matrix class provided by Saddle. It is the equivalent of a two-dimensional array. The Mat instances store their data as contiguous arrays in memory. You can create a Mat object by supplying an array as well as the shape of the matrix. Shape refers to the number of rows and columns in the matrix:

```scala
scala> val m = Mat(2, 3, Array(1, 1, 2, 3, 5, 8))
m: org.saddle.Mat[Int] =
[2 x 3]
1 1 2
3 5 8
```

If you want an identity matrix, an empty matrix, or a matrix filled with zeros, then the following three cases would be of help:

```scala
scala> mat.ident(2)
res0: org.saddle.Mat[Double] =
[2 x 2]
1.0000 0.0000
0.0000 1.0000


scala> mat.ones(2, 2)
res1: org.saddle.Mat[Double] =
[2 x 2]
1.0000 1.0000
1.0000 1.0000


scala> mat.zeros(2, 2)
res2: org.saddle.Mat[Double] =
[2 x 2]
0.0000 0.0000
0.0000 0.0000
```

Creating a matrix with Mat

Finally, you may wish to initialize a matrix with random numbers. This is done similarly to how it is done with the `Vec` class. Use the `rand` method of the singleton object `mat` to get matrices filled with uniformly distributed numbers. The `randn()` method will give you a matrix filled with normally distributed numbers with mean 0.0 and standard deviation 1.0. The `randn2()` method will initialize the matrix with random values from the normal distribution with specified mean and standard deviation:

```scala
scala> mat.rand(2, 2)
res3: org.saddle.Mat[Double] =
[2 x 2]
-0.0017 -0.3253
 0.5774  0.0358


scala> mat.randn(2, 2)
res4: org.saddle.Mat[Double] =
[2 x 2]
-0.2194  0.2507
 0.4389 -0.2572


scala> mat.randn2(2, 2, -2.0, 1.0)
res5: org.saddle.Mat[Double] =
[2 x 2]
-1.4356 -0.1590
-1.6382 -3.1054
```

To get a diagonal matrix, use the `diag()` method. It takes a vector as argument. The values of the vectors will be placed along the diagonal of the resulting matrix. Other elements (ones not on the diagonal) will be set to zero:

```scala
scala> mat.diag(Vec(3, 1))
res6: org.saddle.Mat[Double] =
[2 x 2]
3.0000 0.0000
0.0000 1.0000
```

Applying arithmetic operators in Mat structures

Element-wise arithmetic works the same way with matrices as it does with vectors. Therefore, we will not give examples of it. You simply use arithmetic operators with the Mat instances. The matrices have to have the same shape (the same number of rows and columns). If you have matrices m1 and m2 and apply, say, multiplication operator *m1 * m2*, the result will contain elements of the first matrix multiplied by the corresponding element of the other matrix. Corresponding here means the element on the same row and column. You can calculate the dot product between two matrices using the dot () method. Obviously, the shape of the matrices has to be properly chosen:

```scala
scala> val m1 = Mat(3, 2, Vec(1, 2, 3, 4, 5, 6))
m1: org.saddle.Mat[Int] =
[3 x 2]
1 2
3 4
5 6


scala> val m2 = Mat(2, 3, Vec(6, 5, 4, 3, 2, 1))
m2: org.saddle.Mat[Int] =
[2 x 3]
6 5 4
3 2 1


scala> m1 dot m2
res0: org.saddle.Mat[Double] =
[3 x 3]
12.0000  9.0000  6.0000
30.0000 23.0000 16.0000
48.0000 37.0000 26.0000
```

Using Matrix in the Mat structure

You may also want to get some information about the matrix. This, for example, can include the shape of the matrix. For the matrix m1 defined for the previous example, you can get the number of rows and columns using the numRows and numCols methods:

```scala
scala> m1.numRows
res0: Int = 3
```

```
scala> m1.numCols
res1: Int = 2
```

If you want to get single elements or entire rows and columns from a matrix, see the following few examples. The `at` method returns the element from a specific row and column. The `col()` and `row()` methods return `Vec` corresponding to a specified row or column of a matrix:

```
scala> m1.at(0, 2)
res0: org.saddle.scalar.Scalar[Int] = 3

scala> m1.col(0)
res1: org.saddle.Vec[Int] =
[3 x 1]
1
3
5

scala> m1.row(0)
res2: org.saddle.Vec[Int] =
[2 x 1]
1
2
```

To reshape a matrix, use the `reshape` method that takes a number of rows and columns and transforms the matrix to conform to that shape. We will use the `m1` matrix and swap the number of columns and rows in the following example. The matrix being reshaped has to have the required number of elements. The number of elements has to be the same in the reshaped matrix as in the matrix being reshaped:

```
scala> m1.reshape(2, 3)
res0: org.saddle.Mat[Int] =
[2 x 3]
1 2 3
4 5 6
```

The `Vec` and `Mat` classes are at the base of the more involved Saddle classes such as `Series` and `Frame`. `Series` is a `Vec` where each element is assigned some arbitrary key. In a `Frame` class, each row and column is assigned a key. This will let us work with structured data, and query, transform, and analyze it. How this works exactly we will see in the two following sections.

Series

The `Series` class combines the `Vec` class with an index, the result of which is a kind of key/value mapping. An example could be a simple integer-based indexing of rows. Or, for a more involved example, you could label series of financial data with timestamps. What this means in practice we will see in the next few examples. To construct the `Series` objects, simply specify the keys and provide the value vector. This can be done in several different ways. If you don't specify anything and just provide a vector, then the indices are just natural numbers starting with zero:

```scala
scala> val s = Series(vec.rand(5))
s: org.saddle.Series[Int,Double] =
[5 x 1]
0 -> -0.0780
1 -> -0.3634
2 ->  0.9900
3 ->  0.3414
4 ->  0.9454
```

You can also supply explicit indices by providing tuples with the first element being the key:

```scala
scala> val s = Series('a' -> 1.3, 'b' -> 4.3, 'c' -> 4.8)
s: org.saddle.Series[Char,Double] =
[3 x 1]
a -> 1.3000
b -> 4.3000
c -> 4.8000
```

Alternatively, you can supply the values and the index separately as shown here:

```scala
scala> val s = Series(Vec(1.3, 4.3, 4.8), Index('a', 'b', 'c'))
s: org.saddle.Series[Char,Double] =
[3 x 1]
a -> 1.3000
b -> 4.3000
c -> 4.8000
```

You can use the `at` method to extract an element of the `Series` class corresponding to its place in the value vector (ignoring the index):

```
scala> s.at(1)
res0: org.saddle.scalar.Scalar[Double] = 4.3
```

You can also extract elements by supplying their key:

```
scala> s('b')
res1: org.saddle.Series[Char,Double] =
[1 x 1]
b -> 4.3000
```

You can extract several elements by specifying several keys. If the key is the same for several elements, then all the elements sharing the key will be included. Keys that don't exist (if specified) will be simply ignored:

```
scala> val s = Series(vec.randn(5), Index('a', 'b', 'b', 'c', 'c'))
s: org.saddle.Series[Char,Double] =
[5 x 1]
a ->  -0.3108
b ->   1.4983
b ->   0.4500
c ->  -1.1399
c ->  -0.9405


scala> s('a', 'c')
res0: org.saddle.Series[Char,Double] =
[3 x 1]
a ->  -0.3108
c ->  -1.1399
c ->  -0.9405
```

Implementing the groupBy method in the Series structure

Let's discuss the `groupBy()` method. This is a method with many practical applications. You can use it to group values by their keys. After that, you can combine and transform those values. Alternatively, you may want to do something with the groups directly. This is a very powerful and simple technique useful in a lot of cases in data analysis. You can use it when you want extract information from rows sharing the same key. In the following code snippet, we group the `Series` class we defined previously by their keys and display the results by calling the `groups` method. This method will return an array of tuples where the first element is the key and the second element is an array of elements sharing that key. The elements are represented not directly but by giving their positions in the series:

```scala
scala> val g = s.groupBy
g: org.saddle.groupby.SeriesGrouper[Char,Char,Double] = org.saddle.
groupby.SeriesGrouper@3576592c


scala> g.groups
res0: Array[(Char, Array[Int])] = Array((a,Array(0)), (b,Array(1, 2)),
(c,Array(3, 4)))
```

You can combine the groups. This will apply a function specified as an argument to the `combine` method to each group. The function must take a `Series` object as its argument. For example, we may wonder what the mean of the values in each group is:

```scala
scala> g.combine(_.mean)
res0: org.saddle.Series[Char,Double] =
[3 x 1]
a ->  -0.3108
b ->   0.9742
c ->  -1.0402
```

Applying the transform method in Series

You can also use the `transform` method. The idea behind it is to first group the elements by key and then apply a function to each element in the group. The function takes a `Series` object as its argument and returns whatever type the vector elements are. It should become clearer why this is useful if you consider the following example, where we use `transform` to apply standard score normalization to each group.

Note that in the result, the mean and standard deviation are taken separately for each group, that is, the function supplied to `transform` takes a group as its argument:

```scala
scala> val s = Series('a' -> 12.0, 'a' -> 0.5, 'a' -> 0.3, 'b' -> 32.3,
'b' -> 13.3)
s: org.saddle.Series[Char,Double] =
[5 x 1]
a -> 12.0000
a ->  0.5000
a ->  0.3000
b -> 32.3000
b -> 13.3000


scala> s.groupBy.transform(s1 => (s1 - s1.mean) / s1.stdev)
res0: org.saddle.Series[Char,Double] =
[5 x 1]
a ->  1.1546
a -> -0.5624
a -> -0.5922
b ->  0.7071
b -> -0.7071
```

Using numerical operators in Series

You can use numerical operators on the `Series` objects. These will automatically align data. If a key is missing in one of the `Series` objects, then the value of that row will be NA. For example, see the following two cases:

```scala
scala> val s1 = Series('a' -> 3.0, 'b' -> 3.0, 'c' -> 5.0)
s1: org.saddle.Series[Char,Double] =
[3 x 1]
a -> 3.0000
b -> 3.0000
c -> 5.0000


scala> val s2 = Series('b' -> -3.0, 'c' -> 0.2, 'd' -> 0.5)
s2: org.saddle.Series[Char,Double] =
[3 x 1]
```

```
b -> -3.0000
c ->  0.2000
d ->  0.5000

scala> s1 - s2
res4: org.saddle.Series[Char,Double] =
[4 x 1]
a ->      NA
b -> 6.0000
c -> 4.8000
d ->      NA

scala> s1 / s2
res5: org.saddle.Series[Char,Double] =
[4 x 1]
a ->       NA
b -> -1.0000
c -> 25.0000
d ->       NA
```

Joining Series using the join operation

Finally, you can join two `Series` objects. There are four different `join` operations, each of which will return `Frame`. We will discuss frames later. However, let's examine how the `join` operations work right now.

Applying index.LeftJoin

First of all, `index.LeftJoin` will match the rows in the first `Series` object with the rows in the second `Series` object. If any of the keys are missing in the second object, the result for that key will be NA:

```
scala> s1.join(s2, how=index.LeftJoin)
res0: org.saddle.Frame[Char,Int,Double] =
[3 x 2]
          0        1
     ------ -------
a -> 3.0000      NA
b -> 3.0000 -3.0000
c -> 5.0000  0.2000
```

Applying index.RightJoin

The `index.RightJoin` method will match the rows in the second `Series` object with the rows in the first `Series` object. Again, if any of the rows in the second object are missing in the first one, the result for that key will be NA:

```
scala> s1.join(s2, how=index.RightJoin)
res1: org.saddle.Frame[Char,Int,Double] =
[3 x 2]
          0        1
       ------  -------
b -> 3.0000  -3.0000
c -> 5.0000   0.2000
d ->     NA   0.5000
```

Applying index.InnerJoin

The `index.InnerJoin` method will try to match keys from both `Series`. They will be included in the results if the key is in both the `Series` objects. Think of this as the key-wise intersection of the two `Series` objects:

```
scala> s1.join(s2, how=index.InnerJoin)
res2: org.saddle.Frame[Char,Int,Double] =
[2 x 2]
          0        1
       ------  -------
b -> 3.0000  -3.0000
c -> 5.0000   0.2000
```

Applying index.OuterJoin

The `index.OuterJoin` method will try to match keys from both `Series`. They will be included in the result if the key is present in either of the `Series` objects. Think of this as the key-wise union of the two `Series` objects:

```
scala> s1.join(s2, how=index.OuterJoin)
res3: org.saddle.Frame[Char,Int,Double] =
[4 x 2]
          0        1
       ------  -------
a -> 3.0000      NA
b -> 3.0000  -3.0000
```

```
c -> 5.0000  0.2000
d ->    NA  0.5000
```

You can see the rest of the `Series` API documented at the following website:

```
http://saddle.github.io/saddle/saddle-core/target/scala-2.9.2/api/
org/saddle/Series.html
```

Frame

The `Frame` class is the one you will be using most of the time while using Saddle for data processing and analysis. This is especially true if you are working with structured data. The `Frame` class will be familiar to you if you have worked with pandas or R. In Saddle, it is a matrix where rows and columns get their own indices. This is analogous to how `Series` was constructed with the help of the `Vec` class. The following table is an example using our planets example from the previous chapters. We will see how to convert it to a Saddle Frame and perform various operations on it:

Planets	Mass	Period
Mercury	3.3011E23	0.240864
Venus	4.8675E24	0.615
Earth	5.97237E24	1
Mars	6.4171E23	1.881
Jupiter	1.8986E27	11.86
Saturn	5.6836E26	29.46
Uranus	8.6810E25	84.01
Neptune	1.0243E26	164.8

Here, the row indices are the planet names, while the column indices are the properties of those planets. Alternatively, we could create a separate column for the planet names and let the row index be an increasing integer. Let's see how one would create `Frame` using this data:

```
scala> val mass: Series[String, Double] = Series("Mercury" -> 3.3011E23,
"Venus" -> 4.8675E24, "Earth" -> 5.97237E24, "Mars" -> 6.4171E23,
"Jupiter" -> 1.8986E27, "Saturn" -> 5.6836E26, "Uranus" -> 8.6810E25,
"Neptune" -> 1.0243E26)

mass: org.saddle.Series[String,Double] =

[8 x 1]

Mercury ->      330110000000000000000000.0000
```

```
   Venus ->      486750000000000000000000.0000
   Earth ->      597237000000000000000000.0000
    Mars ->       64171000000000000000000.0000
Jupiter -> 1898600000000000000000000000.0000
 Saturn ->    568360000000000000000000000.0000
 Uranus ->      86810000000000000000000000.0000
Neptune ->    102430000000000000000000000.0000


scala> val period: Series[String, Double] = Series("Mercury" -> 0.240864,
"Venus" -> 0.615, "Earth" -> 1, "Mars" -> 1.881, "Jupiter" -> 11.86,
"Saturn" -> 29.46, "Uranus" -> 84.01, "Neptune" -> 164.8)
period: org.saddle.Series[String,Double] =
[8 x 1]
Mercury ->    0.2409
  Venus ->    0.6150
  Earth ->    1.0000
   Mars ->    1.8810
Jupiter ->   11.8600
 Saturn ->   29.4600
 Uranus ->   84.0100
Neptune ->  164.8000


scala> val planets = Frame("Mass" -> mass, "Period" -> period)
planets: org.saddle.Frame[String,String,Double] =
[8 x 2]
                                            Mass    Period
                 --------------------------------- --------
Mercury ->      33011000000000000000000.0000    0.2409
  Venus ->      486750000000000000000000.0000    0.6150
  Earth ->      597237000000000000000000.0000    1.0000
   Mars ->       64171000000000000000000.0000    1.8810
Jupiter -> 1898600000000000000000000000.0000   11.8600
 Saturn ->    568360000000000000000000000.0000   29.4600
 Uranus ->      86810000000000000000000000.0000   84.0100
Neptune ->    102430000000000000000000000.0000  164.8000
```

You can then form queries much like you would to a SQL database. For example, if I decide I want to get all the planets that are lighter than Earth in terms of mass, we can use the following query (among many other possibilities):

```scala
scala> val lightPlanets = planets.rfilter { case row => row("Mass").first
< 5.97237E24}
lightPlanets: org.saddle.Frame[String,String,Double] =
[3 x 2]

                                    Mass Period
           --------------------------------- ------
Mercury ->   33011000000000000000000.0000 0.2409
  Venus ->   48675000000000000000000.0000 0.6150
   Mars ->   64171000000000000000000.0000 1.8810
```

Here, we use `rfilter` to filter by rows. Only rows for which the result of the supplied function is `true` will be included in the resulting frame. We then get the value, the key of which is `Mass`. We finally extract the `Double` value using the method called `first()`.

We can also extract rows and columns by their index. For example, to extract the planetary periods, you can use it as in the following example. The result here is a `Series` object with the values of that column:

```scala
scala> planets.colAt(1)
res18: org.saddle.Series[String,Double] =
[8 x 1]
Mercury ->   0.2409
  Venus ->   0.6150
  Earth ->   1.0000
   Mars ->   1.8810
Jupiter ->  11.8600
 Saturn ->  29.4600
 Uranus ->  84.0100
Neptune -> 164.8000
```

Using the rowAt method in Frame

You can also extract rows similarly, using the `rowAt()` method. This can be useful in combination with various sorting methods, as this would allow you to select the row that has the *n*th lowest or highest value in some column. See the following example for how we could retrieve the row corresponding to the planet with the fourth smallest period:

```
scala> val sorted = planets.sortedRowsBy { case r => r("Period").first }
sorted: org.saddle.Frame[String,String,Double] =
[8 x 2]

                                            Mass    Period
           -------------------------------- --------
Mercury -> 33011000000000000000000.0000     0.2409
  Venus -> 48675000000000000000000.0000     0.6150
  Earth -> 59723700000000000000000.0000     1.0000
   Mars -> 64171000000000000000000.0000     1.8810
Jupiter -> 18986000000000000000000000.0000  11.8600
 Saturn -> 56836000000000000000000000.0000  29.4600
 Uranus -> 86810000000000000000000.0000     84.0100
Neptune -> 102430000000000000000000.0000   164.8000
```

```
scala> sorted.rowAt(3)
res20: org.saddle.Series[String,Double] =
[2 x 1]
  Mass -> 64171000000000000000000.0000
Period ->                        1.8810
```

Using the sortedColsBy method in Frame

You can also use `sortedColsBy()` to sort columns the same way as we did for rows. All the arithmetic operations that worked on `Series` will similarly work on frames. See the following examples. As you can see, only the columns and rows that are represented in both of the frames are present in the results. The elements which lack a corresponding element in the other matrix will be represented by NA:

```
scala> val f1 = Frame('x' -> Series('a' -> 0.1, 'b' -> 0.2, 'c' -> 0.3),
'y' -> Series('a' -> 0.4, 'b' -> 0.5, 'c' -> 0.6))
f1: org.saddle.Frame[Char,Char,Double] =
[3 x 2]
```

```
          x      y
       ------ ------
a -> 0.1000 0.4000
b -> 0.2000 0.5000
c -> 0.3000 0.6000


scala> val f2 = Frame('y' -> Series('b' -> 0.7, 'c' -> 0.8, 'd' -> 0.9),
'z' -> Series('b' -> 1.0, 'c' -> 1.1, 'd' -> 1.2))
f2: org.saddle.Frame[Char,Char,Double] =
[3 x 2]
          y      z
       ------ ------
b -> 0.7000 1.0000
c -> 0.8000 1.1000
d -> 0.9000 1.2000


scala> f1 * f2
res21: org.saddle.Frame[Char,Char,Double] =
[4 x 3]
        x      y  z
       -- ------ --
a -> NA      NA NA
b -> NA 0.3500 NA
c -> NA 0.4800 NA
d -> NA      NA NA


scala> f1 - f2
res22: org.saddle.Frame[Char,Char,Double] =
[4 x 3]
        x       y  z
       -- ------- --
a -> NA       NA NA
b -> NA -0.2000 NA
c -> NA -0.2000 NA
d -> NA       NA NA
```

There is quite a lot you can do with the `Frame` class. We will not review the remaining methods in detail here. Instead, let's look at an example of how to use the `Frame` class in a more or less practical setting. You can find the full documentation for the `Frame` class by going to the following link:

```
https://saddle.github.io/saddle/saddle-core/target/scala-2.9.3/
api/#org.saddle.Frame
```

Data analysis with Saddle

In this section, let's look through an example of how one would use Saddle for data analysis. In this case, we will use the IRIS dataset again. We used it when discussing data storage and retrieval. You can get the dataset from this website:

```
https://archive.ics.uci.edu/ml/machine-learning-databases/iris/
```

The data is stored in CSV format, where values are separated by commas. Download the the file `iris.data` into the folder you used to test the Saddle examples in this chapter. Values are arranged in rows of five. The first value is sepal length in centimeters, the second value is sepal width in centimeters, the third value is petal length in centimeters, the fourth value is petal width in centimeters, and the fifth value is the name of the flower. The first thing we will want to do is to read the data in to a Saddle Frame. We want a frame where rows are labeled with an integer key and the columns represent one of the five attributes. We will label the columns accordingly.

There are some things to mention first. Since the `Mat` class in Saddle is a matrix containing homogeneous values (values of the same type), we will want to replace the flower names with integers. Just use a text editor to find and replace `Iris-setosa` with `0`, `Iris-versicolor` with `1` and `Iris-virginica` with `2`. This will let us work with these classes while using doubles to represent them. The second point is that the CSV reading facilities in Saddle are a bit fiddly. If there are empty lines at the end of the file, it will fail to read the file correctly since the reader will try to parse five columns from an empty line. Make sure there are no empty lines after the last line. After that, you can try to run the following code:

```scala
import org.saddle._
import org.saddle.io._

object SaddleIris {
  def main(args: Array[String]) {
    val fs = CsvFile("iris.data")
    val data = CsvParser.parse(fs)
```

```
        println(data)
    }
}
```

If everything goes right, you should see the output that is given here. It created a frame where the first four columns are the attribute values and the fifth column is the class index:

```
[150 x 5]
            0   1   2   3   4
          --- --- --- --- --
    0 -> 5.1 3.5 1.4 0.2  0
    1 -> 4.9 3.0 1.4 0.2  0
    2 -> 4.7 3.2 1.3 0.2  0
    3 -> 4.6 3.1 1.5 0.2  0
    4 -> 5.0 3.6 1.4 0.2  0
...
  145 -> 6.7 3.0 5.2 2.3  2
  146 -> 6.3 2.5 5.0 1.9  2
  147 -> 6.5 3.0 5.2 2.0  2
  148 -> 6.2 3.4 5.4 2.3  2
  149 -> 5.9 3.0 5.1 1.8  2
```

There is a slight problem now, due to the fact that the type of the frame above is Frame[Int, Int, String]. This means that the rows and columns have indices that are integers and the values in the frame are all strings. We want the column index to represent attribute names and we want the elements to be double because that will enable us to analyze the data easier. You can use the following code to convert the data frame. Here, we first use mapValues to convert the values in Frame to Double. After that, we create a new Frame class where we use new key columns:

```
val doubleData = data.mapValues { case elt => elt.toDouble }
val irisData = Frame("SepalLength" -> data.colAt(0), "SepalWidth" ->
data.colAt(1), "PetalLength" -> data.colAt(2), "PetalWidth" -> data.
colAt(3), "Class" -> data.colAt(4))
```

Using Breeze with Saddle

One thing we may want to do is plot this data. However, Saddle does not have its own plotting facilities. We will employ the help of Breeze in this case. We will discuss visualization methods in a later chapter. However, we will make a plot now that is called a **matrix plot**. Basically, we will plot each possible pair of attributes against each other. For this, let us first enable the use of Breeze in our program. Add the following lines to the `build.sbt` file:

```
libraryDependencies  ++= Seq(
  "org.scalanlp" %% "breeze" % "0.11.2",
  "org.scalanlp" %% "breeze-natives" % "0.11.2",
  "org.scalanlp" %% "breeze-viz" % "0.11.2"
)
```

Now our project will be able to use the plotting libraries provided by Breeze. Simply import them as shown here:

```
import breeze.plot._
```

The code for doing the matrix plot follows. Let's discuss the details of implementation. First, we create a new figure and specify its width and height:

```
val f = Figure()
f.width = 800
f.height = 800
var c = 0
var i = 0
var j = 0
val columns = Vector("Sepal Length", "Sepal Width",
  "Petal Length", "Petal Width")
val colors = Vector("red", "green", "blue")
```

We will now create a separate subplot for each combination of two attributes. This means 16 subplots in total. We will create scatter plots for attribute pairs when the row and column index of the subplot are not equal and we will create a histogram of the values of that parameter when the row and column indices are equal:

```
val subplots = for (i <- 0 to 3; j <- 0 to 3)
  yield { f.subplot(4, 4, i + 4 * j)  }
```

We will also plot the data for each class separately. As a result of this, each class will get its own color code. Here, we iterate over each combination of class and two attributes and plot the data as a scatter plot in the appropriate subplot. We then label the axes with the attribute names to make sure it is clear what is plotted against what:

```
for (c <- 0 to 2; i <- 0 to 3; j <- 0 to 3; if i != j) {
  val data = irisData.rfilter { case r => r.at(4).toInt == c }
  val xs = for (x <- data.colAt(i).toSeq) yield { x._2 }
  val ys = for (y <- data.colAt(j).toSeq) yield { y._2 }
  val p = subplots(i + 4 * j)
  p += plot(xs, ys, '+')
  p.xlabel = columns(i)
  p.ylabel = columns(j)
}
```

The question remains what to do for the diagonal of the scatter plot matrix. The diagonal would contain plots where attributes are plotted against themselves if the method we employed with the other elements of the matrix was applied. This is not terribly exciting. We will plot the histogram of the values of that attribute instead:

```
for (i <- 0 to 3) {
  val p = f.subplot(4, 4, i + 4 * i)
  val col = for (x <- irisData.colAt(i).toSeq) yield { x._2 }
  p += hist(col, 20)
  p.xlabel = columns(i)
}
f.saveas("matrix.png")
```

Finally, we saved the resulting figure to a file. You can see the following figure:

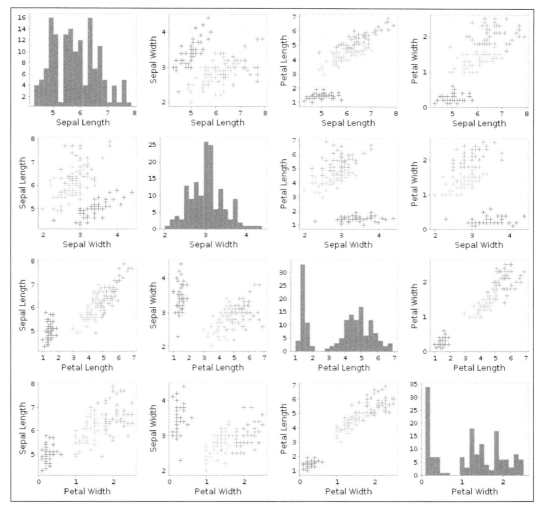

Figure 1

Summary

In this chapter, we considered using the Saddle library for data analysis. Saddle is modeled after the pandas library that is available for Python as well as the R programming language. It has data structures for operations on structured data. We discussed the data types made available by Saddle.

We then examined the operations provided by Saddle that operate on those structures. The basis of most Saddle programs is the `Frame` structure. We discussed operations on it, read data in to it, and performed various queries on it. Finally, we described an example of using Saddle data structures for simple data analysis using visualization.

Interactive Computing with ScalaLab

ScalaLab is an interactive numerical computing environment in the spirit of MATLAB. It let's you create and fill with data vectors and matrices on-the-fly, perform various operations on them, and plot and otherwise interpret the results of those operations. You can then iterate this process to refine the computations depending on what those results are. In practice, this means that you can conveniently import your data, manipulate it, perform computations on it, and then do various things with the resulting data. Alternatively, you can write all that down in a script and run it later.

ScalaLab is written in Java and is thus available for a variety of platforms. ScalaLab is even available for the popular Raspberry Pi computer that is used by scientists, engineers, DIY enthusiasts, and educators worldwide. While it is written in Java, the scripting language it uses is Scala. This is done through the use of an embedded interpreter. As such, you can use all of your Scala skills in a scientific computing context. ScalaLab uses a variant of Scala extended with a **domain specific language** (**DSL**) called **ScalaSci**. In practice, this simply means that data structures relevant to numerical computing and relevant methods are provided once you load the ScalaLab environment. Scala's syntax and other features remain unaffected.

The chapter covers:

- Installing and running ScalaLab
- Basic ScalaSci data structures
- Data storage and retrieval
- Plotting with ScalaLab
- Other ScalaLab features

Installing and running ScalaLab

Currently, and hopefully when you are reading this as well, the website where you can find ScalaLab is the following:

```
https://code.google.com/p/scalalab/
```

You can get the files needed to run ScalaLab from SourceForge. The link is provided here:

```
http://sourceforge.net/projects/scalalab/
```

However, note that there are a lot of files available currently on the download page of ScalaLab. It may be confusing to pick the right one. I suggest downloading the newest file that begins with `ScalaLabAll`. For example, `ScalaLabAllNov15.zip`. The file should be around 160 MB. Download the file on to your hard drive and extract the archive. Open a terminal window and navigate to the directory you extracted the files into. You can then run ScalaLab by executing one of the scripts provided. Exactly which one to execute will depend on what operating system you are using and whether you are on a 32- or 64-bit system. For example, on my Linux laptop, the command is given as follows:

```
$ ./Linux64RunScalaLabServerJVM.sh
```

After running the script, you should see the window shown in the following screenshot. If you are confused as to what to do next, don't worry. We will examine the basics of using ScalaLab soon:

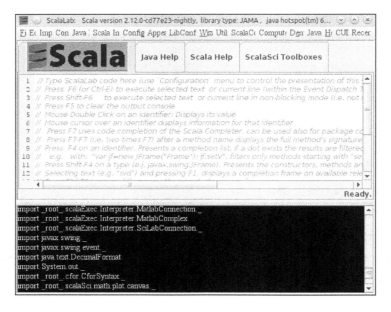

Basic ScalaSci data structures

As mentioned before, ScalaLab uses its own domain-specific language called **ScalaSci**. Just think of it as Scala extended with data structures and methods providing some of the functionality of MATLAB. These include vector and matrix objects as well as various useful methods. They work similarly to how they work in the Breeze and Saddle systems we discussed before.

We will briefly overview them here. Covering all the functionality completely would require a separate book. To start using the functionality, you will need to import it. You can do it as shown here:

```
import scalaSci._
```

Enter the `import` statement into the ScalaLab window. You can execute statements by first selecting them as you would select a block of text in the ScalaLab text editor, and then pressing the *F6* button. Alternatively, you can navigate the cursor to the line you want to execute, and then press *Ctrl + E* (or, depending on your system, a different modifier key + *E*). Try to do this with the preceding `import` statement. You should see output in the console window at the bottom of the ScalaLab screen:

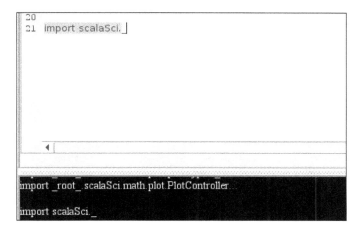

Vector

We looked at more different vector and matrix implementations in this book than you probably would have liked. However, the implementation provided by ScalaLab is different enough to merit at least quickly glancing over it. A lot of it draws inspiration from similar data types in MATLAB. To create a zero-filled vector, simply specify its size:

```
val v = new Vec(10)
```

The output will be displayed in the output section of the ScalaLab window:

```
v: scalaSci.Vec =
0.0000   0.0000   0.0000   0.0000   0.0000   0.0000   0.0000   0.0000   0.0000
0.0000
```

Alternatively, you can specify the elements in line. They have to be supplied as either a space - or comma-separated string of values for some reason:

```
val v1 = V("0 1 2 3")
val v2 = V("0, 1, 2, 3")
```

The preceding two lines are functionally equivalent. Both will create a vector initialized with the same values. The values will be `Double` even though we omitted the decimal point in our definitions:

```
v: scalaSci.Vec =
0.0000   1.0000   2.0000   3.0000
```

Vectors are dynamically resizable. Vector size will be expanded when you append elements or other vectors to it. To get vector size, you can use the `size()` or `length()` methods that are equivalent in functionality:

```
v.length
v.size
```

They will both result in the same value:

```
res0: Int = 10
res1: Int = 10
```

To concatenate two vectors, you can use the `::` and `:::` operators. The only difference between them is that the first one will prepend and the second one will append. See the example of their use here:

```
val v1 = V("1 2 3 4")
val v2 = V("5 6 7 8")
val v3 = v1 :: v2
val v4 = v1 ::: v2
```

The preceding commands, when executed, will result in the following console output:

```
v1: scalaSci.Vec =
1.0000   2.0000   3.0000   4.0000
v2: scalaSci.Vec =
```

```
5.0000   6.0000   7.0000   8.0000
v3:  scalaSci.Vec =
5.0000   6.0000   7.0000   8.0000   1.0000   2.0000   3.0000   4.0000
v4:  scalaSci.Vec =
1.0000   2.0000   3.0000   4.0000   5.0000   6.0000   7.0000   8.0000
```

To append and prepend scalar values to vectors, you can use the `: :`, `: : :`, `: :<`, and `: : :<` operators. These will actually append values by changing the actual vector in-place, instead of creating a new vector:

```
val v5 = 9 :: v1
val v6 = 10 ::: v1
val v7 = v1 ::< 11
val v8 = v1 :::< 12
```

The result of these commands is given here:

```
v5:  scalaSci.Vec =
1.0000   2.0000   3.0000   4.0000   9.0000
v6:  scalaSci.Vec =
10.0000   1.0000   2.0000   3.0000   4.0000   9.0000
v7:  scalaSci.Vec =
10.0000   1.0000   2.0000   3.0000   4.0000   9.0000   11.0000
v8:  scalaSci.Vec =
12.0000   10.0000   1.0000   2.0000   3.0000   4.0000   9.0000   11.0000
```

All of the arithmetic operators come with regular and in-place versions. The `+`, `-`, `*`, and `/` operators will create new vectors. The `++`, `--`, `**`, and `//` operators will perform the operation in place. This means that the values in the vector on the left side of the operator will be replaced by the result of the operation.

To create linearly or logarithmically spaced value vectors use the `linspace(a, b, N)` and `logspace(a, b, N, base)` functions. The arguments to those functions should be self-explanatory:

```
val x1 = linspace(0.0, 1.0, 10)
var x2 = logspace(0.0, 1.0, 10, 10)
```

The result of the above should be:

```
x1: scalaSci.RichDouble1DArray =
0.0000   0.1111   0.2222   0.3333   0.4444   0.5556   0.6667   0.7778   0.8889
1.0000
x2: scalaSci.RichDouble1DArray =
0.0000   0.0801   0.1665   0.2599   0.3608   0.4697   0.5874   0.7145   0.8517
1.0000
```

The inc(a, d, b) function is similar to linspace. Arguments a and b specify the value range, and value d specifies the difference between two adjacent values in the resulting vector:

```
val x = inc(0.0, 0.1, 1.0)


x: scalaSci.Vec =
0.0000   0.1000   0.2000   0.3000   0.4000   0.5000   0.6000   0.7000   0.8000
0.9000   1.0000
```

To get a dot product of two vectors use the dot method:

```
val x1 = V("0 1 2 3")
val x2 = V("4 5 6 7")
val x3 = x1 dot x2
x1: scalaSci.Vec =
0.0000   1.0000   2.0000   3.0000
x2: scalaSci.Vec =
4.0000   5.0000   6.0000   7.0000
x3: Double = 38.0
```

Matrix

To create a matrix filled with zeros, just specify the number of rows and columns:

```
val m1 = Matrix(2, 3)


m1: scalaSci.Matrix =

0.000   0.000   0.000
0.000   0.000   0.000
```

You can also specify the values to initialize the matrix by using a notation similar to that used in MATLAB:

```
val m2 = M1("1 2 3; 4 5 6")
```

```
m2: scalaSci.Matrix =
```

```
1.000   2.000   3.000
4.000   5.000   6.000
```

You can also initialize the matrix with a specific value.

```
val m3 = new Matrix(2, 3, 5.0)
```

```
m3: scalaSci.Matrix =
```

```
5.000   5.000   5.000
5.000   5.000   5.000
```

To select an element of a matrix, you can use the following method:

```
var m = M1("1 2 3; 4 5 6")
m(1, 2)
```

It gives the following output:

```
m: scalaSci.Matrix =
```

```
1.000   2.000   3.000
4.000   5.000   6.000
res2: Double = 2.0
```

The take-home message here is that, like in MATLAB, row and column indices start with one instead of (more common in programming languages) zero. Similarly, you can assign values by specifying the row and column:

```
m(1, 2) = 8
```

```
res2: scalaSci.Matrix =
```

```
1.000   8.000   3.000
4.000   5.000   6.000
```

Other ScalaSci functionality

A plethora of functions work on ScalaSci vectors and matrices. We will not go into detail here, but simply provide a reference so that you know what is available. All of the following take as an argument a single vector or matrix:

- Trigonometric functions: `sin`, `cos`, `tan`, `asin`, `acos`, `asin`, `sinh`, `cosh`, and `tanh`

- Other mathematical functions: `abs`, `ceil`, `floor`, `sqrt`, `log`, and `exp`

- Descriptive statistics: `min`, `max`, `mean`, and `std`

For example, to calculate a value of `sine` for each element of a vector, you can do the following:

```
var v = V("1 2 3 4 5 6")
sin(v)
```

```
res0: scalaSci.Vec =
0.8415  0.9093  0.1411  -0.7568  -0.9589  -0.2794
```

You would use the remaining functions similarly.

There are also simple-to-use, fast Fourier transform routines provided. The `fft` method takes as its only argument a vector. It then returns a tuple containing vectors with real and imaginary parts of the FFT. The inverse Fourier transform is done via the `ifft` method, which takes two arrays, one with real and one with imaginary components as shown here:

```
var v = V("1 2 3 4 5 6 7 8 9 10 11 12 13 14 15 16")
var fft_v = fft(v)
var v_reconstructed = ifft(fft_v._1, fft_v._2)
```

```
v_reconstructed: Array[Double] = Array(1.0000000000000004,
2.0, 2.99999999999999, 3.99999999999999, 4.99999999999999,
5.99999999999999, 6.99999999999999, 8.0, 9.0, 10.0, 11.0, 12.0, 13.0,
14.0, 15.0, 16.0)
```

Data storage and retrieval

It is possible to store ScalaLab arrays as text files. It is also possible to read these files. The file format is very simple. This also lets you create text containing data using any tool you want and load it into ScalaLab as data, as long as you follow the file format that is used, of course. There are two functions for doing this. They are called readAscii and saveAscii. The signatures of those functions are given here:

```
saveAscii(d: Array[Double], fileName: String): Unit
saveAscii(dd: Array[Array[Double]], fileName: String, sepChar:
Char= ' '): Unit
readD1Ascii( fileName: String): Array[Double]
readD2Ascii(fileName: String): Array[Array[Double]]
```

The save function takes an array of doubles and a filename. The data will be stored into the file specified. The other version of the save function takes a 2-dimensional array and saves it to a specified file. You can also supply a separator symbol to be used. The default separator is the space. Let's see how this works:

```
val x = V("1 2 3 4 5")
saveAscii(x.getv, "x.dat")
```

First, we create a vector and then we save it to a file called x.dat. Note that we use the getv method to retrieve an array of doubles from a ScalaLab vector. The resulting file is given here. As you can see, it is simply values separated by spaces:

```
1.0 2.0 3.0 4.0 5.0
```

Similarly, we can store ScalaLab matrices:

```
val m = M1("1 2 3; 4 5 6; 7 8 9; 10 11 12")
saveAscii(m.getv, "m.dat")
```

The resulting file is given here:

```
0.0 0.0 0.0 0.0
0.0 1.0 2.0 3.0
0.0 4.0 5.0 6.0
0.0 7.0 8.0 9.0
0.0 10.0 11.0 12.0
```

We will read it using the `readD2Ascii` method. If we read it back in, we get the following output:

```
var dat = readD2Ascii("m.dat")

dat: Array[Array[Double]] = Array(Array(0.0, 0.0, 0.0, 0.0), Array(0.0,
1.0, 2.0, 3.0), Array(0.0, 4.0, 5.0, 6.0), Array(0.0, 7.0, 8.0, 9.0),
Array(0.0, 10.0, 11.0, 12.0))
```

The preceding four methods should be kept in mind as a simple way of getting your data in and out of ScalaLab conveniently. In other words, it can be used for quick data storage and retrieval.

Plotting with ScalaLab

Plotting is discussed in a separate chapter in this book. However, plotting is a very important part of any interactive computing system. Also ScalaLab is not a Scala library per se. It does own thing but uses Scala as a scripting language. As such, we will discuss ScalaLab's plotting here briefly. Hopefully, this will make explorative computing with ScalaLab much more interesting. Plus, ScalaLab supports a fairly extensive plotting API modeled after MATLAB. An example is shown in the following screenshot:

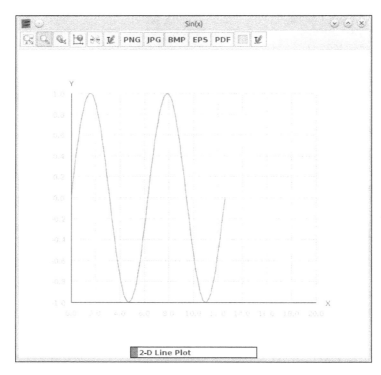

Let's see how to create a simple plot. We use the `plot` method to plot a sinusoid as well as well as the `title` method to set the title of the plot:

```
import scalaSci._

var x = linspace(0.0, 4.0 * PI, 100)
var y = sin(x)
plot(x, y)
```

You will get the plot given in the figure. Let's now explore slightly more advanced plots. For example, the plotting API allows subplots. That is, we can have several different plots in the same figure. For example, we might want to plot a signal using both its time and frequency domain representations as illustrated here:

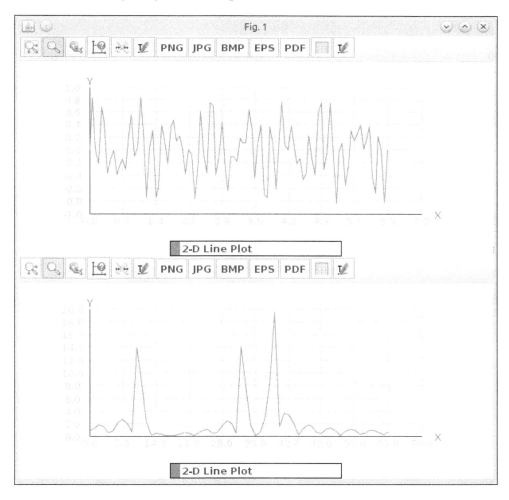

In the following code snippet, we define a signal as a sum of three sinusoids with different frequencies and amplitudes:

```
import scalaSci._

var x = linspace(0.0, 2.0 * PI, 100)
var y1 = 0.3 * sin(8.0 * x)
var y2 = 0.3 * sin(25.0 * x)
var y3 = 0.4 * sin(30.0 * x)
var signal = y1 + y2 + y3
var fft_y = fft(signal)
var fft_abs = sqrt(fft_y._1 * fft_y._1 + fft_y._2 * fft_y._2)
subplot(2, 1, 1)
plot(x, signal)
subplot(2, 1, 2)
plot(fft_abs)
```

Then, we perform an FFT analysis on the signal. We calculate the absolute values of the resulting complex numbers (we will need those to plot the FFT representation). We will want two subplots and divide the screen in two, horizontally. To accomplish this, we use the subplot method. It takes three parameters, the first two of which specify how many rows and columns the resulting plot will have. Here, we specify two rows and one column. This means that there will be two subplots stacked on top of one another, if we specified two rows and three columns.

For example, there would be six subplots arranged into two columns, each having three rows of subplots. The third argument to the subplot method specifies the index of the subplot to draw on. Be aware that indices start with one and not zero. This is a MATLAB convention to help people who are used to the MATLAB way of doing this, I suppose.

It is also possible to perform 3D plots using this system. You need to create a 3D figure and then pass three arguments to the `plot` method:

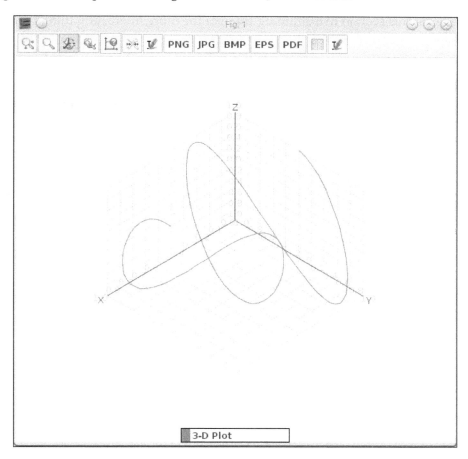

The three arguments are arrays with values for points for each of the three dimensions. This is a direct extension of the 2-dimensional plotting routines:

```
val x = linspace(0.0, 1.0, 100)
val y = sin(x * 4.0 * PI)
val z = cos(x * 6.0 * PI)
figure3d(1)
plot(x, y, z)
```

Other ScalaLab features

To cover everything that is made available via ScalaLab would take a separate book. Let's dedicate this section to examining some of the more interesting things provided by ScalaLab.

Doing symbolic algebra using symja

symja is a symbolic algebra system for Java. It implements the basic functionality one might expect from a symbolic algebra package. For example, you can enter and evaluate expressions, simplify them, calculate derivatives symbolically, and many other things. You can access the symja window from ScalaLab's **ComputerAlgebra | Main symja interface** menu option. It will open the window shown in the screenshot:

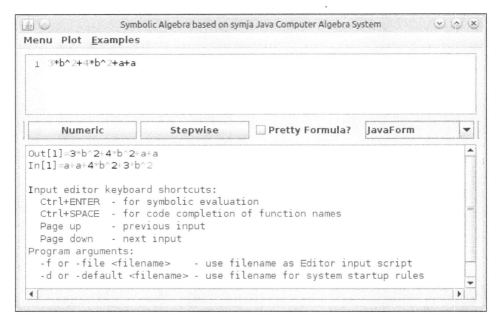

You can enter expressions in the text area that occupies the upper half of the window. The result will be shown in the bottom half area. You can enable LaTeX output by selecting **TeXForm** in the drop-down menu and checking the **Pretty Formula?** checkbox.

We will not go through the functionality provided by symja fully, but let's look at some simple examples that may be useful when performing numerical computing using other Scala packages. For example, you can calculate a derivative of a function. Note that the output window will have input and output lines reversed. This is also evident in the code examples here. Enter the line labeled In[1] in the symja expression window and press the **Symbolic** button:

```
Out[1]=Cos[x^Cos[x]]*(-Log[x]*Sin[x]+Cos[x]*x^(-1))*x^Cos[x]
In[1]=D[Sin[x^Cos[x]],x]
```

Sometimes, you may need to calculate Taylor's series for a given function. You can do it using the built-in Taylor function. It takes an expression, a variable for which the series will be calculated, the point for which the derivatives will be calculated, and finally how many terms to calculate. See the following example:

```
Out[2]=1.3215486790144299E-6*x^8.0+1.525273380405986E-
5*x^7.0+1.5403530393381606E-
4*x^6.0+0.001333355814642847*x^5.0+0.009618129107628473*x^4.0+0.05
550410866482162*x^3.0+0.24022650695910058*x^2.0+0.6931471805599453
*x+1.0
In[2]=Taylor[2.0 ^ x, {x, 0, 8}]
```

It also has plotting functionality, where you can enter symbolic expressions and have them plotted. You can access it via the **Plot** menu option. See the example in the following screenshot:

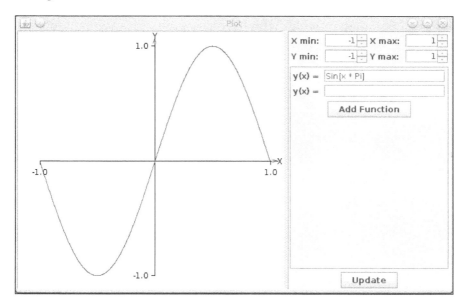

You can carry out many different things with symja; however, the problem is that it is very sparsely documented. The main website is given at the following link:

```
https://code.google.com/p/symja/
```

If you want to go deeper and examine the API and the functionality provided by symja, you should probably look at the API. You can find the functions provided by the symja interpreter here:

```
https://bitbucket.org/axelclk/symja_android_library/wiki/Functions
```

Summary

In this chapter, we provided an overview of ScalaLab—an interactive computing environment written in Java that uses Scala as a scripting language. The Scala interpreter automatically loads various extensions to Scala when ScalaLab is started. For example, classes representing vectors and matrices of doubles are automatically loaded; so are various methods that operate on these data structures.

We provided a quick overview of this functionality. We also explored the plotting facilities provided by ScalaLab. These are modeled after those found in MATLAB, like many things in ScalaLab.

You learned to do simple two-dimensional plots, multiple subplots on the same figure, as well as three-dimensional plots. We then moved to the symbolic algebra capabilities that ScalaLab provides with the help of the symja symbolic algebra package for Java. After reading this chapter, the reader should be able to install and run ScalaLab and perform basic interactive computing tasks with it.

6
Parallel Programming in Scala

Parallel programming (sometimes referred to as **concurrent programming**) refers to executing several processes at the same time. By processes, I mean either operating level processes, threads, or maybe programs on different computers connected in a network. By itself, that does not sound interesting. Simply running several programs at the same time is useful, but it's hard to see what is there to talk about in this book or how it is related to scientific computing. You run them, you get the results, maybe process those results, and so on. Any kinds of complication (and at the same time interesting stuff) only happen when those processes have to interact with each other.

In fact, many algorithms can be written as several processes working together toward a unified goal and exchanging information in order to accomplish that goal. This is particularly attractive at this time when CPUs with multiple cores are widely available, and the clock frequencies of separate cores have stopped increasing. Each process can be executed on a separate CPU core; if they all share workload between them, then the efficiency of a given computing task can be greatly increased.

In the ideal case the computing time would be divided by the number of processes launched. However, in practice, the matter is more complicated, but we won't get into that right now. It should be apparent that parallel programming is something we want to do when confronted by a computationally expensive task. If our task takes 1 hour and 20 minutes to complete, by executing it on eight cores, we can hope to reduce that time to just 10 minutes.

There are several options in Scala for performing parallel programming. First of all, we have standard Java threads that operate similarly to how they do in Java. They have the advantage of being familiar to programmers and intuitively clear to use. However, this low-level approach has the disadvantage of being plagued by synchronization issues unless the programmer is very familiar with the intricacies of parallel programming.

Secondly, we have Scala's own parallel collections. There are parallel versions of the Scala collection classes. These allow for more or less effortless parallelism at the expense of the flexibility provided by the threading approach. And last, but not least, we have the Akka framework. It allows for agent-based concurrency. You will learn about all three approaches in this chapter:

- Programming with Scala threads
- Using Scala's parallel collections
- Agent-based concurrency with the Akka framework

Programming with Scala threads

Scala's threading API uses Java threads. In fact, the wrapper is very thin and they work almost exactly the same way that Java threads do. This is probably the most straightforward way of carrying out parallelism in Scala if you are already familiar with threading APIs in other languages. However, Scala also extends the Java threading API in numerous ways that make it even more convenient to work with. We will look into those ways in this section.

A simple Scala thread example

Let's see a very simple example of programming with Scala threads. The following is the simplest example I could come up with; however, it is also the one that manages to illustrate the most basic uses of the old Java threading model. The following example runs three threads, each of which gets a specific message to print a standard output. The threads are then run in parallel, each printing its message and pausing for one second between printing statements. This will continue until you terminate it (you can terminate it by pressing *Ctrl + C* on UNIX-like systems).

```
class MessageThread(message: String) extends Runnable {
  var msg: String = message

  def run() {
    while (true) {
      println(msg)
```

```
      Thread.sleep(1000)
    }
  }
}

object Threading {
  def main(args: Array[String]) {
    val t1 = new Thread(new MessageThread("hello"))
    val t2 = new Thread(new MessageThread("world"))
    val t3 = new Thread(new MessageThread("!"))
    t1.start
    t2.start
    t3.start
  }
}
```

There are a couple of points that you need to note here. A single thread is represented by a separate Thread object. Each instance of the Thread class is instantiated by passing to it an instance of a class that extends the Runnable trait. Usually, when classes extend this trait, they are meant to be used with the Thread class. At the very minimum, you should override the run method. The body of this method will be executed when a thread is run. In our case, the run method will print the message specified as an argument to the constructor over and over again with a one second pause in between.

After we have instantiated the Thread objects, we call the start method on each of them. Predictably, this will start the thread and call the run method of the Runnable class. It is important to note that the start method does not block. It starts the thread and then the execution of the statements following it in the Scala program is resumed.

At the end of our program, there will be three threads running. A question may arise, since the start methods are non-blocking and there is nothing following them. Why does our program not terminate? The reason is the way Java threads work; the program does not terminate until at least one of its threads is running (unless the thread itself exits the program by calling System.exit() or some other way). If we changed the while loops to terminate after a specific number of iterations, then the program would terminate after the run methods of all threads returned.

Another point to mention. Sometimes you might not want to do anything until all of your threads have finished doing their thing. This usually happens when each thread does a portion of the work and you need all portions to proceed with your calculations. In that case, you can use the join method provided by the Thread class. The join method will block until the thread has finished its work and it's run method has returned. Say for example you have a list of Thread instances called myThreads. Then the parallelization of your program will proceed as shown here:

```
myThreads.foreach(t => t.start())
myThreads.foreach(t => t.join())
```

If the threads take different times to complete, this may lead to performance issues, since the program will have to wait for the slowest thread to finish before proceeding with the results. A way of dealing with this is to manage the workload to threads in a more intelligent way. But this requires implementing some kind of scheduling algorithm and is probably not needed for most applications, especially if you make sure that each thread gets more or less the same amount of work to do in advance.

Synchronization

Everything is fine so far. Running several threads at the same time poses no threats if the threads are independent. The issues start to arise when threads try to access the same variable. To be more precise, if the threads only read from the same memory location that is fine. The same is also true if the threads only write to some memory location (although this second case is rare in practice). Problems start when several threads both read and write to the same memory location (usually a variable) and when two threads access the same object instance.

These issues go by the common name of **race conditions**. Let's consider a simple example of a race condition. For example, two threads try to increment the value of a variable called a by one. Incrementing a variable means reading its value, adding one to that value, and then writing it back. Suppose we have two threads called Thread1 and Thread2. Now consider the following situation, where reading, incrementing, and writing are done in this sequence:

1. Thread1 reads the value of a, which is 7.
2. Thread2 reads the value of a, which is 7.
3. Thread2 writes the value of a incremented by one, which is 8.
4. Thread1 writes the value of a incremented by one, which is 8.

Can you see a problem with this? Since both threads incremented variable a, the value of which was equal to 7, it should now be 9. However, if the operations were done in the preceding sequence, the value of a will be 8, which is clearly incorrect. This is called a race condition.

Race conditions occur when operations have to be performed in a specific order for the result to be correct. However, due to parallelism the order ultimately gets mixed up. We do not know when the thread or process manager will decide to stop one of the threads and start executing another one. As such, we cannot make an assumption that the machine operations constituting threads will be executed in a sensible order. This can be a very big problem if you consider life-critical systems. Race conditions in such cases can even cost human lives, or at best the failure or destruction of expensive machinery. As such, special precautions have to be taken.

In our case, we can make incrementing values an atomic operation. This means that it cannot be interrupted by the thread or process management software. For example, you can add a machine instruction called inc, which will increment a variable and is atomic; that is, it cannot be interrupted during it's execution. This solution, however, is not general enough, and most threading APIs provide special constructs to help programmers address synchronization issues, such as race conditions. Let's look at how it is done in the Scala threading API:

```
object Incrementor {
  var a = 0
  def inc() {
    a = a + 1
  }
}

class IncrementThread extends Runnable {
  def run() {
    for (i <- 0 until 1000) {
      Incrementor.inc()
    }
  }
}

object Threading {
  def main(args: Array[String]) {
    val threads = for (i <- 1 to 5) yield new Thread(new
    IncrementThread)
    for (thread <- threads) { thread.start }
    for (thread <- threads) { thread.join }
    println(Incrementor.a)
  }
}
```

What will this program print? Well, it is impossible to tell. On my system, I have performed five consecutive runs, and these are the values I got: 5000, 4287, 1892, 4147, and 1263. As should be apparent, we cannot make any assumptions about what the result will be. We know that the result should be 5000, but the way this program is written, it can be anything. How can we make sure the program works the way it is supposed to? There are several ways.

The first of these is the synchronized method. This implements a mutex. **Mutex** stands for **mutual exclusion**, and means that whichever thread enters the body of the synchronized code block will own that block and no other thread will be able to enter it. The other threads will block until the mutex is released. If you rewrite the Incrementor object as given here and rerun the program, you will notice that the program now always print 5000, which is the result we want:

```
object Incrementor {
  var a = 0
  def inc() {
    this.synchronized {
      a = a + 1
    }
  }
}
```

This is a nice and simple way to solve the race condition problem. However, it comes at a price. First of all, you will need to identify all the places in your program where race conditions may occur and use synchronized for those code segments. Since this will have to be done by hand, it is susceptible to human error. The bugs that are due to race conditions are incredibly hard to find since the nature of the error is often unpredictable and non-reproducible.

Second of all, there is the issue of efficiency; the other threads will have to wait for their turn with the synchronized block. If there are a lot of synchronized blocks or if the synchronized block is very large, it can damage the efficiency of your parallel program greatly. As such you don't want to use synchronized blocks more often than needed or make them larger than needed.

Monte-Carlo pi calculation

Let's examine how to parallelize a simple algorithm using what you learned so far. The algorithm in question is a simple Monte-Carlo integration. We can use it to calculate the value of *pi* to the required precision.

Let's quickly describe the algorithm and see how we can parallelize it:

1. Draw a sample (x, y) at random so that x and y are within the range *[0.0, 1.0]*.

2. Check if $x2 + y2 < 1$.

3. If it is, increment the variable c that holds the number of points within the circle described by the equation $x2 + y2 = 1$.

4. The area of the circle is $pi\ r^2$. Therefore, the value of *pi* is approximately equal to $4\ c/n$, where n is the number of samples drawn so far.

5. Repeat for as many iterations as you like, starting with step 1. Each iteration will increase the accuracy of the approximation.

A graphical explanation of the method is given in the figure. The points within the circle are colored red, while the points outside the circle are colored blue. The ratio of the area of the quarter circle and square is *pi* divided by four. This can be easily seen from basic math. The approximation of that area ratio is the points sampled so far, divided by the number of points that fall inside the circle:

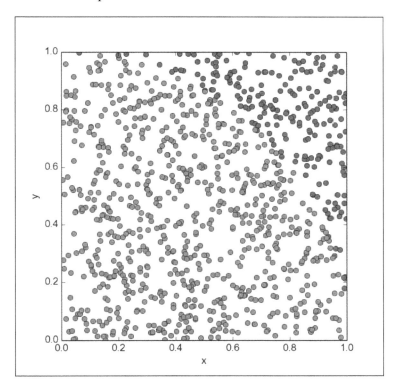

Let's start with a sequential program that implements this method. After that, we will see how we can parallelize it using various different ways. The algorithm itself is not an efficient or sensible way of calculating the approximation to *pi*, but we will let that slide. This is done for illustrative purposes and the algorithm is chosen for it's simplicity:

```scala
import scala.util.Random

object PiSerial {
  def inside(x: Double, y: Double) = {
    x * x + y * y < 1.0
  }

  def main(args: Array[String]) {
    var c = 0.0
    val n = 1000000000
    for (i <- 0 to n) {
      val x = Random.nextDouble
      val y = Random.nextDouble
      if (inside(x, y)) {
        c = c + 1.0
      }
    }
    println(4.0 * (c / n))
  }
}
```

This simple program will print out an approximation of *pi*. The amount of time it takes for the program to complete and the accuracy of the approximation will depend on the value of n. On my system, with the value of n given in the preceding snippet, it can take up to about a minute and the approximation turns out reasonably good:

```
[info] Running PiSerial
3.141561296
[success] Total time: 60 s, completed Dec 6, 2015 10:23:26 PM
```

How can we make use of parallelization in this case? The simplest way would be to simply make several threads, each an instance of this program, and then accumulate data returned by those threads. Generally, this should scale fairly well, since the threads will be fairly independent of one another.

Here, we present the first go at the program. This is a really simple parallel version of the serial program. Note that, because of how cheap the calculations are, the parallelization won't have any appreciable effect on program efficiency. But this is simply because the program is very simple. It is meant merely to show how the parallel program would be done. For more efficiently parallelizable programs, the difference in performance will be apparent on multicode systems. The program code is interspersed with explanations of that code:

```
import java.util.concurrent.Callable
import scala.util.Random

//This will help us keep count of points that fall within the unit //
circle. We need to use synchronized because several threads will //be
incrementing the counter.

object Accumulator {
  var c = 0.0
  def inc() {
    this.synchronized {
      c = c + 1.0
    }
  }
}
```

The `SamplingThread` class extends `Runnable`, will sample random points from the *square (0, 1)2*, and then increment the counter if the sampled point falls within the quarter unit circle. This will be repeated in a loop. The same loop will run in all of the threads:

```
class SamplingThread extends Runnable {
  def run() {
    for (i <- 0 until 500000000) {
      val x = Random.nextDouble
      val y = Random.nextDouble
      if (x * x + y * y < 1.0) {
        Accumulator.inc()
      }
    }
  }
}
```

Finally, we put all the pieces together. We start two threads and use `join` to block until both of them are finished. Then, we print the result out. We have to make sure that we divide by the right thing here. Since there are two threads, we need to multiply the number of loop iterations in each thread by the number of threads:

```
object PiParallel {
  def main(args: Array[String]) {
    var c = 0.0
    val threads = for (i <- 0 until 2) yield { new Thread(new
    SamplingThread) }
    threads.foreach { (thread: Thread) => thread.start }
    threads.foreach { (thread: Thread) => thread.join }
    println(Accumulator.c / (500000000 * 2))
  }
}
```

Using Scala's parallel collections

Scala's parallel collections are a way to provide users with simple and safe tools to perform parallel programming. They come at the expense of reduced generality; however, for a vast number of parallel applications, they will be a simple and sufficient solution. Parallel collections work by providing parallel versions of various Scala collection classes. How that works can be easily seen with an example. First, we import the `ParSeq` class:

```
scala> import scala.collection.parallel.ParSeq
import scala.collection.parallel.ParSeq
```

We then create a list and get it's parallel counterpart. For all collections, this works the same way — by invoking the `par` method on the instance of that collection. The `par` method simply returns a parallel version of that collection. For example, if invoked on a `List` object, it will return the parallel version of `List`. The parallel version acts the same as a regular collection of that type, the only difference being that certain methods acting on that collection will be parallelized:

```
scala> val lst = List(1, 2, 3, 4, 5, 6, 7, 8).par
lst: scala.collection.parallel.immutable.ParSeq[Int] = ParVector(1, 2, 3,
4, 5, 6, 7, 8)
```

We then apply `map` with a desired function. In this case, we simply raise the values in the list to the second power. `map` is a common operation in functional programming languages. It applies a function to every element in a collection and returns a collection with the results of the application. For example, mapping a function that returns a square of it's argument to a collection containing 1, 2, 3, and 4 will produce a collection containing 1, 4, 9, and 16:

```scala
scala> lst.map((x: Int) => x * x)
res0: scala.collection.parallel.immutable.ParSeq[Int] = ParVector(1, 4,
9, 16, 25, 36, 49, 64)
```

You may wonder where parallelism comes in. Well, the version of `map` called here will execute the function passed to it in parallel. This is possible because the different evaluations don't have to know about each other. As there needs to be no communication Scala can automate the concurrent execution of the function. You can similarly use `fold`:

```scala
scala> lst.fold(1)((x: Int, y: Int) => x * y)
res1: Int = 40320
```

Or `filter`:

```scala
scala> lst.filter((x: Int) => x % 2 != 0)
res2: scala.collection.parallel.immutable.ParSeq[Int] = ParVector(1, 3,
5, 7)
```

Or others. A word of caution, however. You will have to make sure that the function you supply to any of these methods does not have any side-effects. That is, it should not modify any variables outside the scope of the function or use I/O routines. Doing so is likely to cause race conditions and other issues and defeats the purpose of using these collections.

The benefits of using parallel collections are likely not very apparent from these examples. To see the benefits, the function used should be more expensive. See the artificially expensive example here:

```scala
import scala.math._

object ParCollections {
  def function(a: Double): Double = {
    var res = 2.0 * Pi * a
    for (i <- 0 until 100000000) {
      res = 2.0 * Pi * sin(res)
    }
    res
  }
```

```
def main(args: Array[String]) {
  val lst = List(0.1, 0.2, 0.3, 0.4, 0.5, 0.6, 0.7, 0.8, 0.9)
  println(lst.map(function))
}
}
```

If I run it on my system with two hyper-threaded CPU cores, I get the following output from SBT:

```
[info] Running ParCollections
List(-1.4482641761481614, 5.671143275310648, -5.895185205207739,
-2.4517773437143235, -4.847082077017533, 6.282512898129773,
-5.671143275310648, 5.895185205207739, 0.5966945087521736)
[success] Total time: 119 s, completed Dec 9, 2015 9:58:23 PM
```

What about the parallel version? All we need to do is import the `ParSeq` class and then add `.par` to the end of our `List` definition so that it looks like the following:

```
val lst = List(0.1, 0.2, 0.3, 0.4, 0.5, 0.6, 0.7, 0.8, 0.9).par
```

This results in a significant performance boost (two-fold) on my system while having to change almost no code in the existing implementation!

```
[info] Running ParCollections
ParVector(-1.4482641761481614, 5.671143275310648, -5.895185205207739,
-2.4517773437143235, -4.847082077017533, 6.282512898129773,
-5.671143275310648, 5.895185205207739, 0.5966945087521736)
[success] Total time: 40 s, completed Dec 9, 2015 10:01:51 PM
```

Agent-based concurrency with the Akka framework

Akka is an agent-based concurrency framework for Scala. It is developed by Typesafe Inc. — the company founded by the creator of the Scala language, Martin Odersky. Therefore, you can be pretty sure that the framework is here to stay. The framework is developed with the goal of simplifying the creation of concurrent programs for the JVM framework.

It is based on the concept of actors communicating by exchanging messages. Each actor will usually run on a separate thread and will abstract some activity that is to be done in parallel. The threading is managed behind the scenes and the writer of the program does not have to worry about low-level details.

It manages to avoid a lot of the issues that plague distributed programming using non-blocking, asynchronous messaging systems. It also supports running programs on clusters. So, your parallel program can work on a super-computing cluster as well as locally on your multicore machine. You can visit the Akka website by visiting the following link:

```
http://akka.io/
```

Akka in effect replaces the previous actor-based concurrency system in Scala. Namely, it replaces the functionality of the `Actor` class that was available in previous Scala versions. Actors are Scala's way of doing (relatively) safe concurrency. They avoid issues such as race conditions and gridlocks by communicating asynchronously via messages.

When a message is passed to an `Actor` class it is stored in it's mail box until `Actor` invokes the `receive` method. They are built around Java threads and generally behave similarly.

Here, we give an example of an actor doing the same kind of calculation we did before with threads. To use the functionality of these new classes, you have to import them first by adding the following to your `build.sbt` file:

```
scalaVersion := "2.11.7"
 libraryDependencies +=
   "com.typesafe.akka" %% "akka-actor" % "2.4-SNAPSHOT"
resolvers += "Akka Snapshot Repository" at
"http://repo.akka.io/snapshots/"
```

From now on, programs that run with `sbt run` will have access to Akka classes we need. Let's see a simple example first. We will take a look at code segments as they come up, so the code is interspersed with comments. First of all, we want to import all the Akka stuff we need. You could use `import akka.actor._`, but let's choose the tidier, if more verbose, approach:

```
import akka.actor.Actor
import akka.actor.ActorSystem
import akka.actor.Props
import akka.actor.ActorRef
```

Instances of the `Actor` class will contain most of the implementation details of your parallel program. Actors can communicate via messages. How to do this we will see shortly. The `ActorSystem` class represents a collection of actors. We will use it as an entry point to create and lookup actors. The `Props` class is a configuration object used to create an actor. Finally `ActorRef` represents an immutable and serializable handle for an actor:

```scala
class PingActor(pong: ActorRef) extends Actor {
  def receive = {
    case "pong" => {
      println("ping")
      pong ! "ping"
    }
  }
}
```

Our first class—the `PingActor` class—takes a reference to a `PongActor` class as an argument to it's constructor. The essence of the class is in the `receive` method that handles messages that this actor receives. Pattern matching is used to invoke different behavior depending on the nature of the message. In our case, the messages are just strings containing `"ping"` and `"pong"`. This class, upon receiving `"pong"`, will print `"ping"` and send `"ping"` to `PongActor`:

```scala
class PongActor extends Actor {
  def receive = {
    case "ping" =>
      println("pong")
      sender ! "pong"
  }
}
```

The second class will receive `"ping"`, print `"pong"`, and send `"pong"` to the sender of the message received. In our case, this will be the `PingActor` instance:

```scala
object TestingAkka {
  def main(args: Array[String]) {
    val system = ActorSystem("PingPongSystem")
    val pongActor = system.actorOf(Props[PongActor], name =
    "pongactor")
    val pingActor = system.actorOf(Props(new
    PingActor(pongActor)), name = "pingactor")
    pingActor ! "pong"
  }
}
```

Finally, it is time to put it all together. We create a new `ActorSystem`, add actors to it, and then launch the whole thing by sending "pong" to `PingActor`. This will cause it to send "ping" to the `PongActor` instance, and the two will continue exchanging messages really quickly until you interrupt it using *Ctrl + C* if you are using a UNIX-like system:

You can look up the API documentation for the preceding classes by going to the following links:

- `http://doc.akka.io/api/akka/2.0/akka/actor/Actor.html`
- `http://doc.akka.io/api/akka/2.0/akka/actor/ActorRef.html`
- `http://doc.akka.io/api/akka/2.0/akka/actor/ActorSystem.html`
- `http://doc.akka.io/api/akka/2.3.1/index.html#akka.actor.Props`

Finally, let us consider our Monte-Carlo pi calculator. Implementing it using Akka actors is trivial and is given in the following program.

Monte-Carlo pi revisited

Let's see how we would implement the Monte-Carlo pi calculator we used in the examples in previous sections. A naïve implementation of that algorithm using actors-based concurrency is presented here.

There are better ways of doing it that we will look into later; but, for the time being, let's just consider what we know so far. For now, just bear in mind that this is simply a direct conversion of the concepts we have used so far in to the format that is used by the Akka framework:

```
import akka.actor.Actor
import akka.actor.ActorSystem
import akka.actor.Props
import akka.actor.ActorRef
import scala.util.Random
```

First, we import all the Akka stuff and the random number generator as well:

```
class PiGenerator(collector: ActorRef) extends Actor {
  def receive = {
    case "request" => {
      val x = Random.nextDouble
      val y = Random.nextDouble
      if (x * x + y * y < 1.0) {
        collector ! "true"
      } else {
```

```
            collector ! "false"
        }
      }
    }
  }
```

The `PiGenerator` object will perform our Monte-Carlo simulation. You can request it to sample the unit square by sending it the message `"request"`. If the point it generates is within the unit circle, it will send the message `"true"` to the `collector` object; otherwise, it will send the message `"false"` to the `collector` object. Depending on those answers, the `collector` object can then estimate how many points fall within the circle and how many fall outside it. From this information, it is then possible to estimate the value of *pi*:

```
class PiCollector extends Actor {
  var counter: Double = 0
  var counterTrue: Double = 0
  def receive = {
    case "true" =>
      counter = counter + 1
      counterTrue = counterTrue + 1
    case "false" =>
      counter = counter + 1
    case "result" =>
      println(4.0 * counterTrue / counter)
  }
}
```

Then, we have the `collector` object. It's job is to listen to messages from generators. When it receives the message `"true"` it will increment the counter used to count points that fall within the unit circle as well as the counter used to count all messages from generators. When it receives `"false"`, it will only increment the counter used to count all messages from generators. Finally, upon receiving the `"result"` message, it will print out the current approximation of *pi*:

```
object PiAkka {
  def main(args: Array[String]) {
    val system = ActorSystem("PiSystem")
    val piCollector = system.actorOf(Props[PiCollector], name =
    "picollector")
    val piGenerators = for (i <- 0 until 4) yield {
      system.actorOf(Props(new PiGenerator(piCollector)), name =
      "pigenerator" + i)
    }
    for (i <- 0 until 1000000) {
```

```
    for (generator <- piGenerators) {
      generator ! "request"
    }
  }
  piCollector ! "result"
  }
}
```

Finally, we glue all the bits together. As before, we initialize the actor system and create the actors. We will need one collector and four generators. You can increase the number of generators depending on how many cores your CPU has. We tell all the generators to use the `collector` object we constructed by passing a reference to it via their constructors. We can simply then send messages to the generators.

The messages are sent to each generator in turn. We do this 1,000,000 times, which means that the unit square will be sampled 4,000,000 times. After all this is done, we send the message that will print the results. This way of doing things is both awkward and error-prone. In fact, there is a bug in the program as it is currently implemented (it will not necessarily affect the operation of this program). But I will let you find it on your own. Let's look at a better version of this program instead.

Using routing

Routing is Akka's way of distributing work to Akka actors. It allows for a more convenient way of doing work scheduling than doing it on your own using ad hoc scheduling strategies. The basic idea is that you implement a routing actor that will route work to worker actors. The routing actor will appear to the other actors as a single worker actor. You simply pass it work and get results.

However, instead of carrying out the work itself, the router will pass work on to one of the workers in it's pool. Which one exactly will depend on the routing strategy you specify. There are several routing strategies supported. Here we give an example of using routing for the Monte-Carlo pi calculator example. We first import the required classes:

```
import akka.actor.Actor
import akka.actor.ActorSystem
import akka.actor.Props
import akka.actor.ActorRef
import akka.routing.ActorRefRoutee
import akka.routing.RoundRobinRoutingLogic
import akka.routing.Router
import scala.util.Random
```

```
case class Work()
case class Inside()
case class Outside()
case class Request()
case class Result(result: Double)
```

This time, instead of using strings for messages, we will use the case classes. This has the advantage that you can use the case classes to pass information of various different types to your actors and return results too. Just use the case class constructor arguments to store the data for the workers and vice versa:

```
class PiCollector extends Actor {
  var counter: Double = 0
  var counterTrue: Double = 0
  def receive = {
    case inside: Inside =>
      counter = counter + 1
      counterTrue = counterTrue + 1
    case outside: Outside =>
      counter = counter + 1
    case request: Request =>
      println(4.0 * counterTrue / counter)
  }
}
```

The collector actor works very similarly to how it worked before. The workers pass messages telling the collector actor whether the point lies inside or outside the unit circle and collector increments the appropriate counters. If it receives a message of type Request it will print out the result:

```
class PiGenerator(collector: ActorRef) extends Actor {
  def receive = {
    case w: Work => {
      val x = Random.nextDouble
      val y = Random.nextDouble
      if (x * x + y * y < 1.0) {
        collector ! Inside()
      } else {
        collector ! Outside()
      }
    }
  }
}
```

As before, the generator samples the unit square and calculates whether the random point lies within the unit circle. Depending on the result of the test, an instance of one of the two `case` classes (`Inside` or `Outside`) is sent to `collector`:

```
class PiRouter(collector: ActorRef) extends Actor {
    var counter: Double = 0
    var counterTrue: Double = 0

  var router = {
    val routees = Vector.fill(4) {
      val r = context.actorOf(Props(new PiGenerator(collector)))
      context watch r
      ActorRefRoutee(r)
    }
    Router(RoundRobinRoutingLogic(), routees)
  }

  def receive = {
    case w: Work =>
      router.route(w, sender())
  }
}
```

This time, we also need a router. The point of a router is to distribute work to worker actors. The `receive` method is therefore simple; upon getting an instance of the `Work` class, dispatch it to one of the routees. You can also send back the result that the routee (worker) returns. To do that, replace the `router.route(w, sender())` line with the following:

```
sender ! router.route(w, sender())
```

We will see how the sender can reliably receive these messages in the next section when we look at the `ask` operator. For the time being, we simply send work to workers. The workers will in turn send data to the `collector`. The key point in the preceding code snippet is the construction of the `Router` object. A `Router` class takes a collection of `ActorRef` instances. These are your worker actors. It also takes a router configuration instance. In this case, it is `RoundRobinRoutingLogic()`, which means that work will be passed to actors in a round-robin fashion — each getting one turn and then waiting until everyone else has had their turn.

Other configurations are presented in the following table:

Class	Description
RoundRobinRoutingLogic	Routing is performed in a round-robin fashion. Each routee gets it's turn and then has to wait until everyone else has had their turn.
RandomRoutingLogic	Randomly selects a routee to send the message to.
SmallestMailboxRoutingLogic	Will attempt to send a message to the routee that has the smallest number of messages in it's mailbox.
BroadcastRoutingLogic	Sends the message to all routees.
ScatterGatherFirstCompletedRoutingLogic	Sends the message to all routees. Then replies with the first response from the routees.
TailChoppingRoutingLogic	Sends the message to a routee picked at random. Waits for a specified interval, sends the message to a different random route, and continues until it has been sent to all the routees. Then repeats the cycle.
ConsistentHashingRoutingLogic	Selects the routee based on the message. Hashing is used to achieve this. Look for more details in the Akka API. This logic is too involved to be covered here.

```
object PiAkka {
  def main(args: Array[String]) {
    val system = ActorSystem("PiSystem")
    val piCollector = system.actorOf(Props[PiCollector], name =
    "picollector")
    val piRouter = system.actorOf(Props(new
    PiRouter(piCollector)), name = "pirouter")
    for (i <- 0 until 1000000) {
      piRouter ! Work()
    }
    Thread.sleep(10000)
    piCollector ! Request()
  }
}
```

The rest of the program is almost exactly the same as before. We create the collector and the router, then we give work to the router which will dispatch it to the workers. We block for 10 seconds to make sure all the threads have finished, and then print the results.

Waiting for a reply

Very often you will begin to feel limited by the completely asynchronous nature of the message passing API that Akka provides. The simplest way to see this is in the preceding example, where we called `Thread.sleep` to wait until the threads had finished calculating. This is not the best (or even a good) way of doing it. The correct way would be to wait for the reply using the Scala `Future` instance that is returned when you use the `?` operator on an Akka actor. You can then use `Await` to block until the result is returned. A short outline of how this can generally be done is given here:

```
import akka.pattern.ask
import akka.util.Timeout
import scala.concurrent.{Await, ExecutionContext, Future}
import scala.concurrent.duration._

val system = ActorSystem("System")
val worker = system.actorOf(Props[Worker], name="rastrigin")
implicit val timeout = Timeout(5 seconds)
val future = worker ? Work()
val result = Await.result(future,
timeout.duration).asInstanceOf[Result]
```

We ask the worker for a reply using the ask operator `?` and then use the `Future` object it returns to block until the result is returned or until a specified timeout is reached. The `Worker` class has to return the result it has produced using the sender actor reference that is defined by the `Actor` class when it is done doing it's share of the work:

```
class Worker extends Actor {
  def receive = {
    case w: Work =>
      // Do work with w to obtain result
      sender ! result
  }
}
```

Summary

In this chapter, we covered the different ways that are available if you want to perform parallel programming in Scala. The ways covered are: using JVM threading primitives, Scala's parallel collections, and the Akka framework.

The JVM threading primitives give a low-level access to the threading capabilities of JVM, but are prone to various problems inherent in most such threading API's. We saw how to write simple programs using the Thread class and how to avoid race conditions via the use of the synchronized statement.

We then explored Scala's parallel collections — parallelized versions of most collection classes. These work by executing various functional programming operations in parallel. Examples include, map, fold, and so on.

We saw how one can use this to very simply parallelize programs that use large collections and rely on functional programming operators. Finally, we scratched the surface of the massive Akka framework for actor-based concurrent programming. The framework works by abstracting functionality as work to be performed by actors that communicate via messages. Since the messaging is fully asynchronous, it avoids a lot of the problems inherent in distributed computation.

We explored writing simple programs in Akka, passing messages between actors, and getting results back through the use of the Future objects. After reading this chapter, you should be on track to start writing your first parallel programs in Scala.

7
Cluster Computing Using Scala

Very often when dealing with intense data processing tasks and simulations of physical phenomena, there comes a time when no matter how many CPU cores and memory your workstation has, it is not enough. At times like these, you will want to turn to supercomputing clusters for help. These distributed computing environments consist of many nodes (each node being a separate computer) connected into a computer network using specialized high bandwidth and low latency connections (or if you are on a budget, standard Ethernet hardware is often enough).

These computers usually utilize a network filesystem allowing each node to see the same files. They communicate using messaging libraries, such as MPI. Your program will run on separate computers and utilize the message passing framework to exchange data via the computer network.

In this chapter, we will look into two ways of writing software to be run on distributed computing clusters. The first one is the MPJ Express library and the second one is the Akka framework we have already met in the previous chapter:

- Using MPJ Express for distributed computing
- Using an Akka cluster for distributed computing

Using MPJ Express for distributed computing

MPJ Express is a message passing library for distributed computing. It works in programming languages using Java Virtual Machine (JVM). So, we can use it from Scala. It is similar in functionality and programming interface to MPI. If you know MPI, you will be able to use MPJ Express pretty much the same way. The differences specific to Scala are explained in this section. We will start with how to install it. For further reference, visit the MPJ Express website given here:

```
http://mpj-express.org/
```

Setting up and running MPJ Express

The steps to set up and run MPJ Express are as follows:

1. First, download MPJ Express from the following link. The version at the time of writing is 0.44:

   ```
   http://mpj-express.org/download.php
   ```

2. Unpack the archive and refer to the included README file for installation instructions. Currently, you have to set MPJ_HOME to the folder you unpacked the archive to and add the bin folder in that archive to your path. For example, if you are a Linux user using bash as your shell, you can add the following two lines to your .bashrc file (the file is in your home directory at /home/yourusername/.bashrc):

   ```
   export MPJ_HOME=/home/yourusername/mpj
   export PATH=$MPJ_HOME/bin:$PATH
   ```

3. Here, mpj is the folder you extracted the archive you downloaded from the MPJ Express website to. If you are using a different system, you will have to do the equivalent of the above for your system to use MPJ Express. We will want to use MPJ Express with Scala Build Tool (SBT), which we used previously to build and run all of our programs. Create the following directory structure:

   ```
   scalacluster/
       lib/
       project/
           plugins.sbt
       build.sbt
   ```

4. I have chosen to name the project folder `scalacluster` here, but you can call it whatever you want. The `.jar` files in the `lib` folder will be accessible to your program now. Copy the contents of the `lib` folder from the `mpj` directory to this folder. Finally, create empty `build.sbt` and `plugins.sbt` files. Let's now write and run a simple `"Hello, World!"` program to test our setup:

```
import mpi._

object MPJTest {
  def main(args: Array[String]) {
    MPI.Init(args)
    val me: Int = MPI.COMM_WORLD.Rank
    val size: Int = MPI.COMM_WORLD.Size
    println("Hello, World, I'm <" + me + ">")
    MPI.Finalize()
  }
}
```

This should be familiar to everyone who has ever used MPI.

First, we import everything from the `mpj` package. Then, we initialize MPJ Express by calling `MPI.Initialize`; the arguments to MPJ Express will be passed from the command-line arguments you will enter when running the program.

The `MPI.COMM_WORLD.Rank()` function returns the MPJ process's rank. A **rank** is a unique identifier used to distinguish processes from one another. They are used when you want different processes to do different things. A common pattern is to use the process with rank 0 as the master process and the processes with other ranks as workers.

Then, you can use the process's rank to decide what action to take in the program. We also determine how many MPJ processes were launched by checking `MPI.COMM_WORLD.Size`. Our program will simply print a processes rank for now. We will want to run it.

If you don't have a distributed computing cluster readily available, don't worry. You can test your programs locally on your desktop or laptop. The same program will work without changes on clusters as well.

To run programs written using MPJ Express, you have to use the `mpjrun.sh` script. This script will be available to you if you have added the `bin` folder of the MPJ Express archive to your `PATH` as described in the section on installing MPJ Express. The `mpjrun.sh` script will set up the environment for your MPJ Express processes and start said processes. Because we want to use this script to run our program, we cannot simply do `sbt run`, like we did with the programs we wrote in previous chapters.

The `mpjrun.sh` script takes a `.jar` file, so we need to create one. Unfortunately for us, this cannot easily be done using the `sbt package` command in the directory containing our program. This worked previously, because we used Scala runtime to execute our programs. MPJ Express uses Java.

The problem is that the `.jar` package created with `sbt package` does not include Scala's standard library. We need what is called a `fat .jar` — one that contains all the dependencies within itself. One way of generating it is to use a plugin for SBT called `sbt-assembly`. The website for this plugin is given here:

```
https://github.com/sbt/sbt-assembly
```

5. There is a simple way of adding the plugin for use in our project. Remember that `project/plugins.sbt` file we created? All you need to do is add the following line to it (the line may be different for different versions of the plugin; consult the website):

```
addSbtPlugin("com.eed3si9n" % "sbt-assembly" % "0.14.1")
```

6. Now, add the following to the `build.sbt` file you created:

```
lazy val root = (project in file(".")).
  settings(
    name := "mpjtest",
    version := "1.0",
    scalaVersion := "2.11.7"
  )
```

7. Then, execute the `sbt assembly` command from the shell to build the `.jar` file. The file will be put under the following directory if you are using the preceding `build.sbt` file, that is, if the folder you put the program and `build.sbt` in is `/home/you/cluster`:

```
/home/you/cluster/target/scala-2.11/mpjtest-assembly-
1.0.jar
```

8. Now you can run the `mpjtest-assembly-1.0.jar` file as follows:

```
$ mpjrun.sh -np 4 -jar target/scala-2.11/mpjtest-assembly-1.0.jar
MPJ Express (0.44) is started in the multicore configuration
Hello, World, I'm <0>
Hello, World, I'm <2>
Hello, World, I'm <3>
Hello, World, I'm <1>
```

Argument `-np` specifies how many processes to run. Since we specified `-np 4`, four processes will be started by the script. The order of the `"Hello, World"` messages can differ on your system since the precise order of execution of different processes is undetermined. If you got an output similar to the one shown here, then congratulations, you have done the majority of the work needed to write and deploy applications using MPJ Express.

Using Send and Recv

MPJ Express processes can communicate using `Send` and `Recv`. These methods constitute arguably the simplest and easiest to understand mode of operation that is also probably the most error-prone. We will look at these two first. The following are the signatures for the `Send` and `Recv` methods:

```
public void Send(java.lang.Object buf, int offset, int count,
Datatype datatype, int dest, int tag) throws MPIException

public Status Recv(java.lang.Object buf, int offset, int count,
Datatype datatype, int source, int tag) throws MPIException
```

Both of these calls are blocking. This means that after calling `Send`, your process will block (will not execute the instructions following it) until a corresponding `Recv` is called by another process. Also `Recv` will block the process, until a corresponding `Send` happens. By corresponding, we mean that the `dest` and `source` arguments of the calls have values corresponding to receiver's and senders, ranks, respectively.

The two calls will be enough to implement many complicated communication patterns. However, they are prone to various problems such as deadlocks. Also, they are quite difficult to debug, since you have to make sure that each `Send` has the correct corresponding `Recv` and vice versa.

The parameters for `Send` and `Recv` are basically the same. The meanings of those parameters are summarized in the following table:

Argument	Type	Description
Buf	`java.lang. Object`	It has to be a one-dimensional Java array. When using from Scala, use the Scala array, which is a one-to-one mapping to a Java array.
offset	`int`	The start of the data you want to pass from the start of the array.
Count	`int`	This shows the number of items of the array you want to pass.

Argument	Type	Description
datatype	Datatype	The type of data in the array. Can be one of the following: MPI.BYTE, MPI.CHAR, MPI.SHORT, MPI.BOOLEAN, MPI.INT, MPI.LONG, MPI.FLOAT, MPI.DOUBLE, MPI.OBJECT, MPI.LB, MPI.UB, and MPI.PACKED.
dest/ source	int	Either the destination to send the message to or the source to get the message from. You use the rank of the process to identify sources and destinations.
tag	int	Used to tag the message. Can be used to introduce different message types. Can be ignored for most common applications.

Let's look at a simple program using these calls for communication. We will implement a simple master/worker communication pattern:

```
import mpi._
import scala.util.Random

object MPJTest {
  def main(args: Array[String]) {
    MPI.Init(args)
    val me: Int = MPI.COMM_WORLD.Rank()
    val size: Int = MPI.COMM_WORLD.Size()
    if (me == 0) {
```

Here, we use an `if` statement to identify who we are based on our rank. Since each process gets a unique rank, this allows us to determine what action should be taken. In our case, we assigned the role of master to the process with rank 0 and the role of worker to processes with other ranks:

```
for (i <- 1 until size) {
  val buf = Array(Random.nextInt(100))
  MPI.COMM_WORLD.Send(buf, 0, 1, MPI.INT, i, 0)
  println("MASTER: Dear <" + i + "> please do work on " +
          buf(0))
}
```

We iterate over workers who have ranks from 1 to whatever is the argument for the number of processes you passed to the `mpjrun.sh` script. Let's say that number is four. This gives us one master process and three worker processes. So, each process with a rank from 1 to 3 will get a randomly generated number. We have to put that number in an array even though it is a single number. This is because both `Send` and `Recv` methods expect an array as their first argument. We then use the `Send` method to send the data. We specified the array as argument `buf`, offset of 0, size of 1, type `MPI.INT`, destination as the `for` loop index, and tag as 0. This means that each of our three worker processes will receive a (most probably) different number:

```
for (i <- 1 until size) {
  val buf = Array(0)
  MPI.COMM_WORLD.Recv(buf, 0, 1, MPI.INT, i, 0)
  println("MASTER: Dear <" + i + "> thanks for the reply,
          which was " + buf(0))
}
```

Finally, we collect the results from the workers. For this, we iterate over the worker ranks and use the `Recv` method on each one of them. We print the result we got from the worker, and this concludes the master's part. We now move on to the workers:

```
} else {
  val buf = Array(0)
  MPI.COMM_WORLD.Recv(buf, 0, 1, MPI.INT, 0, 0)
  println("<" + me + ">: " + "Understood, doing work on " +
          buf(0))
  buf(0) = buf(0) * buf(0)
  MPI.COMM_WORLD.Send(buf, 0, 1, MPI.INT, 0, 0)
  println("<" + me + ">: " + "Reporting back")
}
```

The worker code is identical for all of them. They receive a message from the master, calculate the square of it, and send it back:

```
    MPI.Finalize()
  }
}
```

After you run the program, the results should be akin to the following, which I got when running this program on my system:

```
MASTER: Dear <1> please do work on 71

MASTER: Dear <2> please do work on 12

MASTER: Dear <3> please do work on 55
```

```
<1>: Understood, doing work on 71
<1>: Reported back
MASTER: Dear <1> thanks for the reply, which was 5041
<3>: Understood, doing work on 55
<2>: Understood, doing work on 12
<2>: Reported back
MASTER: Dear <2> thanks for the reply, which was 144
MASTER: Dear <3> thanks for the reply, which was 3025
<3>: Reported back
```

Sending Scala objects in MPJ Express messages

Sometimes, the types provided by MPJ Express for use in the Send and Recv methods are not enough. You may want to send your MPJ Express processes a Scala object. A very realistic example of this would be to send an instance of a Scala case class.

These can be used to construct more complicated data types consisting of several different basic types. A simple example is a two-dimensional vector consisting of x and y coordinates. This can be sent as a simple array, but more complicated classes can't. For example, you may want to use a case class like the one shown here. It has two attributes of type String and one attribute of type Int. So what do we do with a data type like this? The simplest answer to that problem is to serialize it.

Serializing converts an object to a stream of characters or a string that can be sent over the network (or stored to a file or done other things with) and later on deserialized to get the original object back:

```
scala> case class Person(name: String, surname: String, age: Int)
defined class Person


scala> val a = Person("Name", "Surname", 25)
a: Person = Person(Name,Surname,25)
```

A simple way of serializing is to use a format such as XML or JSON. This can be done automatically using a pickling library. **Pickling** is a term that comes from the Python programming language. It is the automatic conversion of an arbitrary object into a string representation that can later be de-converted to get the original object back. The reconstructed object will behave the same way as it did before conversion. This allows one to store arbitrary objects to files, for example.

There is a pickling library available for Scala as well. You can of course do serialization in several different ways (for example, using the powerful support for XML available in Scala).

We will use the pickling library that is available from the following website for this example:

```
https://github.com/scala/pickling
```

You can install it by adding the following line to your `build.sbt` file:

```
libraryDependencies += "org.scala-lang.modules" %% "scala-
pickling" % "0.10.1"
```

After doing that, use the following `import` statements to enable easy pickling in your projects:

```
scala> import scala.pickling.Defaults._
import scala.pickling.Defaults._


scala> import scala.pickling.json._
import scala.pickling.json._
```

Here you can see how you can then easily use this library to pickle and unpickle arbitrary objects without the use of annoying boilerplate code:

```
scala> val pklA = a.pickle
pklA: pickling.json.pickleFormat.PickleType =
JSONPickle({
"$type": "Person",
"name": "Name",
"surname": "Surname",
"age": 25
})
scala> val unpklA = pklA.unpickle[Person]
unpklA: Person = Person(Name,Surname,25)
```

Let's see how this would work in an application using MPJ Express for message passing. A program using pickling to send a `case` class instance in a message is given here:

```
import mpi._
import scala.pickling.Defaults._
import scala.pickling.json._

case class ArbitraryObject(a: Array[Double], b: Array[Int],
c: String)
```

Here we have chosen to define a fairly complex `case` class, consisting of two arrays of different types and a string:

```
object MPJTest {
  def main(args: Array[String]) {
    MPI.Init(args)
    val me: Int = MPI.COMM_WORLD.Rank()
    val size: Int = MPI.COMM_WORLD.Size()
    if (me == 0) {
      val obj = ArbitraryObject(Array(1.0, 2.0, 3.0), Array(1, 2,
                               3), "Hello")
      val pkl = obj.pickle.value.toCharArray
      MPI.COMM_WORLD.Send(pkl, 0, pkl.size, MPI.CHAR, 1, 0)
```

In the preceding bit of code, we create an instance of our `case` class. We then pickle it to JSON and get the string representation of said JSON with the `value` method. However, to send it in an MPJ message, we need to convert it to a one-dimensional array of one of the supported types. Since it is a string, we convert it to a char array. This is done using the `toCharArray` method:

```
    } else if (me == 1) {
      val buf = new Array[Char](1000)
      MPI.COMM_WORLD.Recv(buf, 0, 1000, MPI.CHAR, 0, 0)
      val msg = buf.mkString
      val obj = msg.unpickle[ArbitraryObject]
```

On the receiving end, we get the raw char array, convert it back to string using the `mkString` method, and then unpickle it using `unpickle[T]`. This will return an instance of the `case` class that we can use as any other instance of a `case` class. It is, in its functionality, the same object that was sent to us:

```
      println(msg)
      println(obj.c)
    }
    MPI.Finalize()
  }
}
```

The following is the result of running the preceding program. It prints out the JSON representation of our object, and also shows that we can access the attributes of said object by printing the c attribute.

MPJ Express (0.44) is started in the multicore configuration:

```
{
"$type": "ArbitraryObject",
"a": [
    1.0,
    2.0,
    3.0
  ],
"b": [
    1,
    2,
    3
  ],
"c": "Hello"
}
Hello
```

You can use this method to send arbitrary objects in an MPJ Express message. However, this is just one of many ways of doing this. As mentioned previously, an example of another way is to use XML representation. XML support is strong in Scala, and you can use it to serialize objects as well. This will usually require you to add some boilerplate code to your program to serialize to XML. The method discussed earlier has the advantage of requiring no boilerplate code.

Non-blocking communication

So far, we have examined only blocking (or synchronous) communication between two processes. This means that the process is blocked (its execution halted) until the Send or Recv methods have been completed successfully. This is simple to understand and enough for most cases. The problem with synchronous communication is that you have to be very careful otherwise deadlocks may occur.

Deadlocks are situations when processes wait for each other to release a resource first. Mexican standoff including the dining philosophers problem is one of the famous example of *Deadlock in Operating System*. The point is that if you are unlucky, you may end up with a program that is seemingly stuck and you don't know why.

Using non-locking communication allows you to avoid these problems most of the time. If you think you may be at risk of deadlocks, you will probably want to use it. The signatures for the primary methods used in asynchronous communication are given here:

```
Request Isend(java.lang.Object buf, int offset, int count,
Datatype datatype, int dest, int tag)
```

Isend works similar to its Send counterpart. The main differences are that it does not block (the program continues execution after the call rather than waiting for a corresponding send), and then it returns a Request object. This object is used to check the status of your Send request, block until it is complete if required, and so on:

```
Request Irecv(java.lang.Object buf, int offset, int count, Datatype
datatype, int src, int tag)
```

Irecv is again the same as Recv only non-blocking and returns a Request object used to handle your receive request. The operation of these methods can be seen in action in the following example:

```scala
import mpi._

object MPJTest {
  def main(args: Array[String]) {
    MPI.Init(args)
    val me: Int = MPI.COMM_WORLD.Rank()
    val size: Int = MPI.COMM_WORLD.Size()
    if (me == 0) {
      val requests = for (i <- 0 until 10) yield {
        val buf = Array(i * i)
        MPI.COMM_WORLD.Isend(buf, 0, 1, MPI.INT, 1, 0)
      }
    } else if (me == 1) {
      for (i <- 0 until 10) {
        Thread.sleep(1000)
        val buf = Array[Int](0)
        val request = MPI.COMM_WORLD.Irecv
(buf, 0, 1, MPI.INT, 0, 0)
        request.Wait()
        println("RECEIVED: " + buf(0))
      }
    }
    MPI.Finalize()
  }
}
```

This is a very simplistic example used simply to demonstrate the basics of using the asynchronous message passing methods. First, the process with rank 0 will send 10 messages to the process with rank 1 using `Isend`. Since `Isend` does not block, the loop will finish quickly and the messages it sent will be buffered until they are retrieved using `Irecv`.

The second process (the one with rank 1) will wait for 1 second before retrieving each message. This is to demonstrate the asynchronous nature of these methods. The messages are in the buffer waiting to be retrieved. Therefore, `Irecv` can be used at your leisure when convenient. The `Wait()` method of the `Request` object it returns has to be used to retrieve results. The `Wait()` method blocks until the message is successfully received from the buffer.

Scatter and Gather

There is a more convenient method of distributing work to workers, then iterating over ranks and manually sending messages using `Send` and gathering the results using `Recv`. The `Scatter` method takes an array and distributes the elements to processes based on their rank.

A process will get an element of the array so that the elements' index corresponds to the process rank. The process with rank 0 will get the first element of the array and so on. The signature of the method is given here. The arguments are similar to the ones used by `Send` and `Recv`. The only thing that may need explaining is the difference between `sendbuf` and `recvbuf` arguments. Here, `sendbuf` is the array that contains data to be distributed to the processes. This array is filled by the root process (traditionally, the process with rank 0).

The `recvbuf` argument is the array that each process executes locally to receive the elements distributed by `Scatter`. Let's say you want to distribute elements of a 10-element array to 10 processes. Then, the size of `sendbuf` will be `10`, and the size of `recvbuf` will be `1`:

```
public void Scatter(java.lang.Object sendbuf, int sendoffset, int
sendcount, Datatype sendtype, java.lang.Object recvbuf, int
recvoffset, int recvcount, Datatype recvtype, int root) throws
MPIException
```

The `Gather` method is the reverse of the `Scatter` method. It takes the local arrays that the processes have filled and collects them into an array for the root process to further process. The parameters are the same as for `Scatter`. We will see how `Scatter` and `Gather` will work together when we examine the following example:

```
public void Gather(java.lang.Object sendbuf, int sendoffset, int
sendcount, Datatype sendtype, java.lang.Object recvbuf, int
recvoffset, int recvcount, Datatype recvtype, int root) throws
MPIException
```

Let's look at a simple example. We fill an array with cubes of numbers from 0 to 7 and then scatter them to eight processes. Each process will then double the number it has received and return the result back using `Gather`:

```scala
import mpi._

object MPJTest {
  def main(args: Array[String]) {
    MPI.Init(args)
    val me: Int = MPI.COMM_WORLD.Rank()
    val size: Int = MPI.COMM_WORLD.Size()
    var gdata: Array[Int] = Array.fill(8){0}
    var ldata: Array[Int] = Array(0)
```

We created two arrays. The first one (`gdata`) is to be filled by the root process with work that has to be distributed to other processes. This array will be the same size as the number of processes launched. The second array (`ldata`) will contain a different value for each process. That value is the element of `gdata` with an index corresponding to that process's rank:

```scala
if (me == 0) {
  for (i <- 0 until 8) {
    gdata(i) = i * i * i
  }
}
```

Above, the root process fills the `gdata` array with the squares of numbers from 0 to 7:

```scala
MPI.COMM_WORLD.Scatter(gdata, 0, 1, MPI.INT, ldata, 0, 1,
MPI.INT, 0)
```

The `gdata` array is then scattered. Note that `Scatter` has to be called by every process, not just by the root process. This ensures that `ldata` will contain the required value. If you don't call `Scatter` then `ldata` will remain as it was initialized:

```scala
println("I am <" + me + "> and I have received " + ldata(0))
ldata(0) = ldata(0) * 2
```

Each process will then perform work on its `ldata` array. In this case, it involves simply doubling the value. It will also print the value so that you can see that each process indeed gets a different value in the `ldata` array:

```
    MPI.COMM_WORLD.Gather(ldata, 0, 1, MPI.INT, gdata, 0, 1,
MPI.INT, 0)
```

Again, each process and not only root has to call `Gather` for the results to be assembled back. The arguments for `Gather` are the same as for `Scatter`, only the arrays have switched places. This is because `ldata` will be sent to the root process and received in its proper place in the `gdata` array:

```
    if (me == 0) {
        println("I am MASTER, I have received " + gdata.mkString(""))
    }
```

At the end, we print the array that the root process has gathered from the results sent by the other processes:

```
    MPI.Finalize()
    }
}
```

On my system, after running the program, I get the following output. The processes receive the cubes of numbers, multiply them by 2, and return the result to the root process. The steps contributing to this process are printed to the screen:

```
I am <1> and I have received 1
I am <3> and I have received 27
I am <7> and I have received 343
I am <0> and I have received 0
I am <6> and I have received 216
I am <5> and I have received 125
I am <2> and I have received 8
I am <4> and I have received 64
I am MASTER, I have received 0 2 16 54 128 250 432 686
```

There are some other methods for collective communication that are worth mentioning. These are briefly described as follows:

```
    public void Bcast(java.lang.Object buf, int offset, int count,
    Datatype type, int root) throws MPIException
```

The `Bcast` method will send the same data to all of the processes. This is short-hand and the more effective version of using `Send` to send the same data to all of the processes. The processes will then have to use `Bcast` as well to receive data. Therefore, each process will have to call it. This is similar to how the `Scatter` and `Gather` methods work. The `Allgather` method works the same way as `Gather`, except that all processes receive the result and not just the root process.

```
public void Allgather(java.lang.Object sendbuf, int sendoffset,
int sendcount, Datatype sendtype, java.lang.Object recvbuf, int
recvoffset, int recvcount, Datatype recvtype) throws MPIException
```

You can find the equivalents of the other MPI methods in the MPJ Express API documentation. The link to the API documentation is provided here:

`http://www.mpj-express.org/docs/javadocs/index.html`

Setting up MPJ Express on clusters

The procedure described here will probably work on most clusters and assumes very little about the cluster configuration. If the cluster you are using has already provided the MPJ Express setup, then you don't have to do anything else. Run `mpjrun.sh` using the `-dev native` option.

If the cluster you are using does not have the MPJ Express setup, then you will have to install it by yourself. The following are the steps you need to follow to get MPJ Express running on a cluster. You would then run programs using MPJ Express as you usually run MPI programs:

1. **Install MPJ Express locally**: The installation procedure will be the same as the one described at the beginning of this chapter. You do not need administrative privileges for any of the installation steps.

2. **Compile and install the Java Native Interface (JNI) wrapper**: JNI is part of the **Java Development Kit (JDK)** for interfacing with C/C++ code from JVM. It is included with MPJ Express, but you need to compile and install it. For this, you will need CMake, so make sure you have installed it. You need to perform the following six steps:

```
$ cd $MPJ_HOME/src/mpjdev/natmpjdev/
$ mkdir build
$ cd build
$ cmake ..
$ make
$ make install
```

3. **Run your MPJ Express program**: Use the following command:

```
mpjrun.sh -np 4 -dev native ClassName
```

You can then use your cluster's batch system to submit jobs. You can do this the same way you submit any MPI job, except in this case you would substitute mpirun with mpjrun.sh in the batch script. All of the above assumes that some implementation of MPI is installed on the cluster in question. This will be the case in almost every cluster imaginable.

Using an Akka cluster for distributed computing

It is possible to get Akka actors running on remote hosts. For more information about Akka, refer to the chapter on parallel programming in Scala. Here, we will only consider how you would use Akka in a networked cluster environment. For example, you can easily refer to actors running on a remote actor system:

```
val ref = system.actorOf(FooActor.props.withDeploy(
Deploy(scope = RemoteScope(address))))
```

To find a remote actor (one running on a different computer), you have to use the following pattern:

```
akka.<protocol>://<actorsystemname>@<hostname>:<port>/<actor path>

ActorSelection selection = context.actorSelection(
"akka.tcp://app@10.0.0.1:2552/user/serviceA/worker");
```

After getting the selection, you can use it as you would do for any other actor: send messages, receive messages, and so on. You need to carry out some basic setup for using remoting. For more information about remoting, refer to the remoting section in the following documentation:

```
http://doc.akka.io/docs/akka/snapshot/java/remoting.html
```

Full coverage of the Akka cluster configuration and deployment is well beyond the scope of this chapter. However, you can refer to the excellent documentation prepared by the developer of Akka and Scala and Typesafe Inc. Just go to the following link:

```
http://doc.akka.io/docs/akka/snapshot/java/cluster-usage.html
```

Summary

Extremely computationally intensive programs are usually parallelized and run on supercomputing clusters. These clusters consist of multiple networked computers. Communication between these computers is usually done using messaging libraries such as MPI. These allow you to pass data between processes running on different machines in an efficient manner.

In this chapter, you have learned how to use MPJ Express—an MPI-like library for JVM. We saw how to carry out process-to-process communication as well as collective communication. Most importantly MPJ Express primitives were covered and example programs using them were given.

We also have seen how to deploy MPJ Express programs on clusters. Also, a brief overview of the possibilities of using Akka on clusters was given. Upon reading this chapter, the reader should have a clear idea about how to proceed with writing programs for distributed computing environments and how to translate their knowledge of MPI to solutions available from Scala.

8
Scientific Plotting with Scala

Plotting is often the most convenient and quickest way of analyzing data. Visualizing your data can give you all sorts of insights into what you are dealing with. Common plots, such as histograms, scatter plots, bar plots, and box-and-whisker plots, are often invaluable tools for exploratory statistical analysis.

In this chapter, we will explore several options for dealing with plotting in Scala. We will see how to do the most basic plots with all of them. There are many popular libraries for plotting. Examples include matplotlib, seaborn for Python, and ggplot2 for the R programming language. There aren't as many options for Scala as there are for languages that have been around longer. Those that are available are not as powerful as the ones we mentioned, but they certainly are solid options to get you started. We will look at several good ones you can use.

First of all, there is the JFreeChart library for Java. This is not Scala-specific, and this API does not take advantages of Scala's advanced features. It has been around for a relatively long time. However, this API can produce many different types of plots. It also works well with the Swing GUI framework, which can be an advantage.

Then, we will look into the scala-chart library, which is a Scala wrapper for JFreeChart and allows you to use more idiomatic Scala with it. We will also examine the very convenient Wisp library and how you can use it for scientific plotting.

At the end of this chapter, you should be well on your way to creating professional-quality plots using Scala. In this chapter, we will cover the following topics:

- Plotting with JFreeChart
- Plotting with scala-chart
- Plotting with Wisp

Plotting with JFreeChart

JFreeChart is a very popular open source library for plotting written in Java. It is not specifically designed with scientific plotting in mind. However, you can easily do most types of common scientific plots with it. The advantage of using this library is that it is very well supported and has been around for a longtime. This means that it is probably not going anywhere soon, which is a risk with many of the newer libraries that may not have the required developer power to keep going.

Using JFreeChart in your project

To use JFreeChart in your project, you need to download it and then put it in the `lib` directory of your project. Download JFreeChart by going to the following website:

```
http://www.jfree.org/jfreechart/
```

After downloading the `.zip` file containing the library, copy the `lib` folder from the archive to the `lib` folder under your project tree. This will make the library available to your Scala program when you run it using SBT. Without further ado, let's examine a simple program that uses JFreeChart to plot sine and cosine values against their argument:

```scala
import org.jfree.chart._
import org.jfree.data.xy._
import scala.math._
```

Here, we import JFreeChart stuff as well as mathematical functions and constants we will need for the program:

```scala
object ScalaPlotting {
  def main(args: Array[String]) {
    val x: Array[Double] = Array.tabulate(20) {
      (i: Int) => -Pi + 2.0 * Pi * (i / 20.0)
    }
    val sin_y = x.map(sin(_))
    val cos_y = x.map(cos(_))
```

We will plot the argument *x* that ranges from *-pi* to *+pi* (we sample 20 uniform values in that range) against the values of *sin(x)* and *cos(x)*. The values are being stored in Scala arrays:

```
val dataset = new DefaultXYDataset
dataset.addSeries("sin", Array(x, sin_y))
dataset.addSeries("cos", Array(x, cos_y))
```

We then create a dataset. Dataset instances contain the data that plotting functions will plot. These data series are named, which will help us when adding legends to the plot:

```
val frame = new ChartFrame("Trigonometry",
  ChartFactory.createScatterPlot("Trigonometry", "x", "y",
  dataset, org.jfree.chart.plot.PlotOrientation.VERTICAL,
  true, false, false))
frame.pack()
frame.setVisible(true)
}
}
```

Finally, we create our plot and make it visible. This library works with Swing so you can add plots to Swing user interface elements. We will not be doing this in this chapter, however. We will be using content by showing the plot in it own window or saving it to a file. This concludes our program. You now know how to create a simple scatter plot with JFreeChart, complete with axis labels, plot description, and a legend. The signature of the createScatterPlot method is given here:

```
public static JFreeChart createScatterPlot(
  java.lang.String title, // plot title
  java.lang.String xAxisLabel, // x axis label
  java.lang.String yAxisLabel, // y axis label
  XYDataset dataset, // dataset to plot
  PlotOrientation orientation, // how to orient the plot
  boolean legend, // will we want to display the legend?
  boolean tooltips, // will we want tooltips?
  boolean urls) // adds urls to your plots
```

Here is the output of the mentioned code:

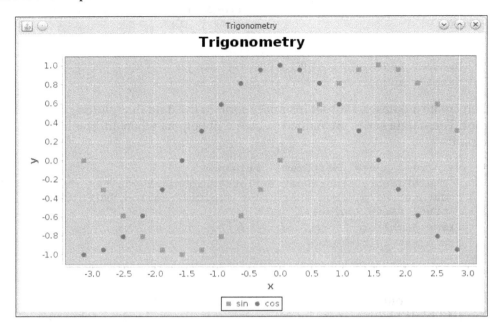

Creating a line plot

With small modifications to the original program, you can create a line plot instead of a scatter plot. Simply use the following method of `ChartFactory` instead of `createScatterPlot` that was used in the previous program:

```
val frame = new ChartFrame("Trigonometry",
  ChartFactory.createXYLineChart("Trigonometry", "x", "y",
  dataset, org.jfree.chart.plot.PlotOrientation.VERTICAL,
  true, false, false))
```

The arguments and their meaning are the same as with `createScatterPlot`.

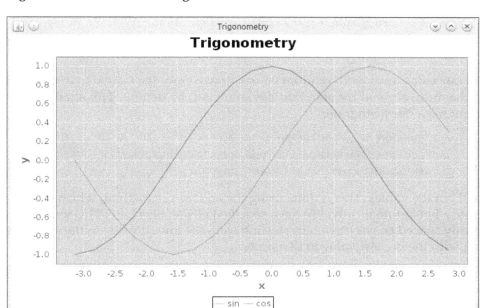

Creating a histogram

Similarly, it is very easy to create histograms with JFreeChart. To create a histogram, you first need a series of numbers. Then, bins are specified. **Bins** are simply value intervals. They can be uniformly spaced. They also have to be consecutive and non-overlapping. Usually, the start of the first interval coincides with the smallest value of the series and the end of the last interval corresponds to the largest value in the series. The idea is to count how many values in your series of numbers fall in each bin. It can serve as a simple visual estimate of the probability distribution of your data.

As mentioned before, you can get a histogram using JFreeChart in much the same way as the plots we did previously. There is just one extra step that has to be done first. That one extra step you have to take is binning the data first. Luckily for us, there is a convenient method for doing just that. Let's look at the following simple histogram example:

```
import org.jfree.chart._
import org.jfree.data.statistics._
import scala.util.Random
```

```
object ScalaPlotting {
  def main(args: Array[String]) {
    val x: Array[Double] = Array.tabulate(1000) {
      (i: Int) => Random.nextGaussian()
    }
```

We fill our value array with random values drawn from the Gaussian distribution. Here, the mean is 0 and the standard deviation is 1, by default. This should then be apparent from our histogram:

```
val dataset = new HistogramDataset();
dataset.setType(HistogramType.RELATIVE_FREQUENCY);
dataset.addSeries("Histogram", x, 11);
```

We will bin the values. This is done using the addSeries method, which will generate a bin automatically. We have specified eleven bins here. This means eleven uniformly spaced consecutive bins starting from the lowest value in the array x and ending with the highest value in that array.

JFreeChart, to the best of my knowledge, does not support manually specified bin values. If you want that functionality, you would have to use your own binning procedure and create a bar chart using values obtained from that binning procedure:

```
val frame = new ChartFrame("Histogram",
  ChartFactory.createHistogram("Histogram", "value",
  "frequency",
    dataset, org.jfree.chart.plot.PlotOrientation.VERTICAL,
    true, false, true))
frame.pack()
frame.setVisible(true)
  }
}
```

The rest of the program is the same, except we use the createHistogram method of ChartFactory. The arguments for this method have the same meaning as in the earlier plotting examples.

The different possible histogram types are given in the following table. These will not affect the look of the histogram, only the values displayed on the vertical axis (if vertical orientation is chosen):

Value	Meaning
HistogramType.FREQUENCY	The height of the bars represents how many samples fall within a bin.
HistogramType.RELATIVE_FREQUENCY	The height of the bars represents the relative frequency (percentage) of values within that bin with regard to the number of samples.
HistogramType.SCALE_AREA_TO_1	The area occupied by the bars will be scaled to add up to 1.

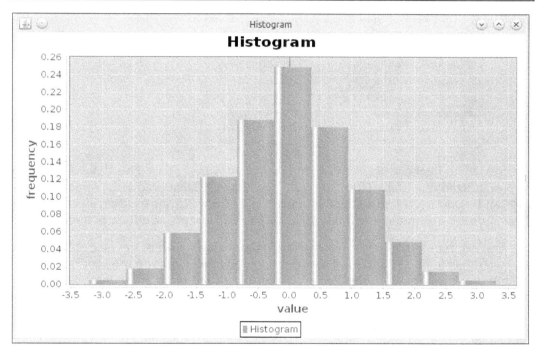

Creating a bar chart

Let's see now how we can create a bar chart. It is a simple chart where the height of a bar represents a numerical value. The idea is that seeing the bars next to each other will let you visually estimate what the ratio between those values is. This is often useful when presenting very simple comparisons between measurements or changes over broad ranges of time. An example program that produces a bar chart is given here:

```scala
import org.jfree.chart._
import org.jfree.data.category._

object ScalaPlotting {
  def main(args: Array[String]) {
    val dataset = new DefaultCategoryDataset();
    dataset.setValue(6, "Q1", "Elbonia");
    dataset.setValue(7, "Q2", "Elbonia");
    dataset.setValue(8, "Q3", "Elbonia");
    dataset.setValue(5, "Q4", "Elbonia");
    dataset.setValue(5, "Q1", "Latveria");
    dataset.setValue(8, "Q2", "Latveria");
    dataset.setValue(7, "Q3", "Latveria");
    dataset.setValue(6, "Q4", "Latveria");
```

We created an instance of the `DefaultCategoryDataset` class. This dataset contains data organized in a table. Think of it as a spreadsheet. Data is added using `addValue` and can be updated or added using `setValue`. Here we can use either, since our dataset does not contain any data, so `setValue` will simply add data to the dataset.

The first argument to `setValue` is the numerical value we want to associate with the bar (it has to be a number), the second argument is the row name, and the third argument is the column name. Each data sample added using these methods will represent a separate bar in the chart. There will be two groups of bars in our case. They will be grouped by the column name. There will be four bars in the set. I made up some "economics" data for demonstration purposes. Each bar represents the made-up country's GDP growth for that quarter:

```scala
val frame = new ChartFrame("GDP Growth",
  ChartFactory.createBarChart("GDP Growth", "Country",
    "GDP Growth (%)", dataset,
    org.jfree.chart.plot.PlotOrientation.VERTICAL,
    true, false, true))
frame.pack()
frame.setVisible(true)
  }
}
```

Creating the plot works the same way it did for all of the other plots we have considered so far. The final result can be seen in the following graph:

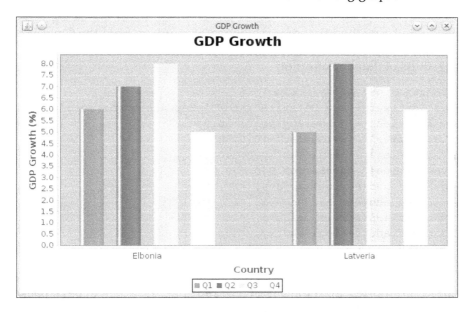

Creating a box-and-whisker chart

Box-and-whisker plots represent groups of numerical data by their quartiles. The line in the middle of each box represents the median. The lower and upper bounds of the box represent the first and third quartiles, respectively. The horizontal lines that are connected to the box by the vertical lines can represent several things. For example, they can denote the lowest and highest value in the group, or the standard deviation.

Outliers are usually displayed as separate points. Refer to the figure at the end of this section to see what all of this means in practice. For the time being let's get straight to the code. The following program produces a box-and-whisker chart:

```
import org.jfree.chart._
import org.jfree.data.statistics._
import scala.collection.JavaConverters._
import scala.util.Random

object ScalaPlotting {
  def getSeries(mean: Double, stddev: Double):
    List[Double] = {
    List.tabulate(20) {
```

```
      (i: Int) => Random.nextGaussian() * stddev + mean
  }
}
```

We implemented a method that draws a bunch of numbers from the Gaussian distribution, scales them, and collects them into a Scala list. This will be used to create groups of data for our plot:

```
def main(args: Array[String]) {
  val dataset = new DefaultBoxAndWhiskerCategoryDataset();
  val series1 = getSeries(20.0, 50.0)
  val series2 = getSeries(-10.0, 20.0)
  val series3 = getSeries(10.0, 40.0)
  val series4 = getSeries(0.0, 30.0)
  dataset.add(series1.asJava, "1", "1")
  dataset.add(series2.asJava, "2", "2")
  dataset.add(series3.asJava, "3", "3")
  dataset.add(series4.asJava, "4", "4")
```

We assemble our groups into a dataset that can be used with the `createBoxAndWhiskerChart` method. Note the use of the `asJava` method here. This method is imported from the `scala.collection.JavaConverters` package. These calls are necessary since the dataset expects us to supply it with data via Java lists rather than Scala lists. Therefore, we need to explicitly convert the lists into something a Java library such as JFreeChart would understand. Luckily, the aforementioned package is designed for this very purpose:

```
val frame = new ChartFrame("Experimental Data",
  ChartFactory.createBoxAndWhiskerChart(
    "Experimental Data",
    "Experiment No.", "Value",
    dataset, false))
frame.pack()
frame.setVisible(true)
  }
}
```

Finally, we create our plot in much the same way we created the others. The `createBoxAndWhiskerChart` method takes fewer arguments than other methods of the `ChartFactory` class we used. See the following signature of the method. The arguments should be mostly self-explanatory:

```
public static JFreeChart createBoxAndWhiskerChart(java.lang.String
title,
  java.lang.String categoryAxisLabel,
  java.lang.String valueAxisLabel,
```

```
BoxAndWhiskerCategoryDataset dataset,
boolean legend)
```

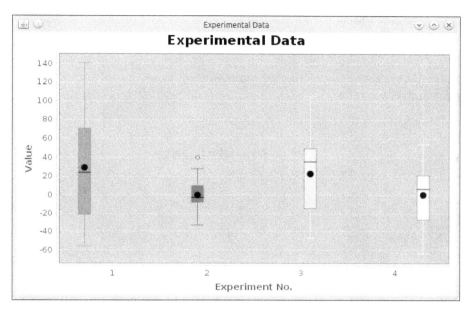

Other plot types

JFreeChart supports several other plot types. However, they are mostly of use in business and financial applications. These include pie charts and the like. We chose not to cover them here. If you want to see the full range of different chart possibilities, refer to the official JFreeChart documentation. The link to the documentation is provided here:

```
http://www.jfree.org/jfreechart/api/javadoc/org/jfree/chart/
ChartFactory.html
```

Saving charts to a file

It is easy to save your plots to a file in the necessary format with JFreeChart. To do this, instead of creating and displaying a Swing frame, we can create a chart and use on it one of the methods meant for saving plots to a file. For example, you can modify the previous program by changing the lines that create the plot with the following:

```
val chart = ChartFactory.createBoxAndWhiskerChart(
  "Experimental Data",
  "Experiment No.", "Value",
```

```
      dataset, false)
  val file = new File("test.png")
  ChartUtilities.saveChartAsPNG(file, chart, 500, 300)
```

You will also need to import the `ChartUtilities` and `java.io.File` classes. You can do so with the `import` statements given here:

```
  import org.jfree.chart.ChartUtilities
  import java.io.File
```

The result is shown in the following screenshot:

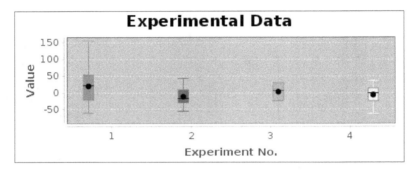

Plotting with scala-chart

scala-chart is a wrapper for JFreeChart that provides a more convenient interface for working with JFreeChart than using the Java library directly. It allows you to accomplish everything that JFreeChart does with fewer lines of code and at the same time using idiomatic Scala, a definite feel-good factor. In this section, we will see how to replicate the plots from the previous section using this library. The website for scala-chart is given here:

```
https://github.com/wookietreiber/scala-chart
```

Installing scala-chart

Create a `build.sbt` file in your project directory like we have done through most of this book. Then, add the following lines to it to pull-in the required dependencies:

```
  libraryDependencies += "com.github.wookietreiber" %% "scala-chart"
  % "latest.integration"
  libraryDependencies += "com.itextpdf" % "itextpdf" % "5.5.6"
  libraryDependencies += "org.jfree" % "jfreesvg" % "3.0"
```

The last two lines will let you export your plots to the PDF and SVG formats. PDF is especially important since you will probably want to use it when exporting plots for use in publications.

After doing this, you can just run your program using `sbt run`.

Creating a line plot

Here, we see a program that will create a line plot that looks exactly the same as the one created using JFreeChart directly. We used it that way in the previous section:

```
import scala.math._
import scalax.chart.api._
import scalax.chart.XYChart

object ScalaPlotting {
  def trig_data(fn: Double => Double) = {
    for (i <- 0 until 20) yield {
      val x = -Pi + 2.0 * Pi * (i / 20.0)
      val y = fn(x)
      (x, y)
    }
  }

  def main(args: Array[String]) {
    val sin_data = trig_data(sin)
    val cos_data = trig_data(cos)
    val data = List("sin" -> sin_data, "cos" -> cos_data)
    val chart = XYLineChart(data, title="Trigonometry")
```

The first important difference here is that we don't have to mess with datasets directly, which reduces the amount of boilerplate code. Instead, the methods that construct our plots take idiomatic Scala collections.

Here, `XYLineChart` takes several data series, each contained in a Scala list. The names of series in the list are mapped to arrays of type `Array[(Double, Double)]`. The arrays contain tuples where the first number is the x value and the second argument is the y value. This is very nice because it means you will be able to quickly plot your data without worrying about transforming it so that JFreeChart accepts it:

```
chart.plot.getDomainAxis().setLabel("x")
chart.plot.getRangeAxis().setLabel("y")
```

Another important difference is that you have to manually set axis labels. For that, you need to get the underlying JFreeChart plot object from your chart and then do the method calls:

```
        chart.show()
    }
}
```

Then just one more line to display your plot on the screen. We will not give the plot itself here to save space since it is exactly the same as the one in the previous section.

Creating a histogram

Here is the code for producing a histogram using scala-chart. This time there are a few significant differences to the JFreeChart version. You still have to use the `HistogramDataset` class from JFreeChart. The example is pretty self-explanatory, so we will leave it uncommented:

```
import scalax.chart.api._
import scala.util.Random
import org.jfree.data.statistics._

object ScalaPlotting {
  def main(args: Array[String]) {
    val x: Array[Double] = Array.tabulate(1000) {
      (i: Int) => Random.nextGaussian()
    }
    val dataset = new HistogramDataset();
    dataset.setType(HistogramType.FREQUENCY);
    dataset.addSeries("Histogram", x, 11);
    val chart = XYBarChart(dataset, title="Histogram",
    legend=false)
    chart.plot.getDomainAxis().setLabel("Value")
    chart.plot.getRangeAxis().setLabel("Frequency")
    chart.show()
  }
}
```

Creating a bar chart

The differences between JFreeChart and the scala-chart version are again fairly minimal. Please see the following program. It should be clear enough without needing additional explanation:

```scala
import scalax.chart.api._
import org.jfree.data.category._

object ScalaPlotting {
  def main(args: Array[String]) {
    val dataset = new DefaultCategoryDataset();
    dataset.setValue(6, "Q1", "Elbonia");
    dataset.setValue(7, "Q2", "Elbonia");
    dataset.setValue(8, "Q3", "Elbonia");
    dataset.setValue(5, "Q4", "Elbonia");
    dataset.setValue(5, "Q1", "Latveria");
    dataset.setValue(8, "Q2", "Latveria");
    dataset.setValue(7, "Q3", "Latveria");
    dataset.setValue(6, "Q4", "Latveria");
    val chart = BarChart(dataset, title="GDP Growth")
    chart.plot.getDomainAxis().setLabel("Country")
    chart.plot.getRangeAxis().setLabel("GDP Growth (%)")
    chart.show()
  }
}
```

Creating a box-and-whisker chart

For completeness, the scala-chart version of our earlier box-and-whisker chart program is included here. It is very similar to the previous one. Examine the following code:

```scala
import org.jfree.data.statistics._
import scala.collection.JavaConverters._
import scala.util.Random
import scalax.chart.api._

object ScalaPlotting {
  def getSeries(mean: Double, stddev: Double): List[Double] = {
    List.tabulate(20) {
      (i: Int) => Random.nextGaussian() * stddev + mean
    }
  }
```

```
    def main(args: Array[String]) {
      val dataset = new DefaultBoxAndWhiskerCategoryDataset();
      val series1 = getSeries(20.0, 50.0)
      val series2 = getSeries(-10.0, 20.0)
      val series3 = getSeries(10.0, 40.0)
      val series4 = getSeries(0.0, 30.0)
      dataset.add(series1.asJava, "1", "1")
      dataset.add(series2.asJava, "2", "2")
      dataset.add(series3.asJava, "3", "3")
      dataset.add(series4.asJava, "4", "4")
      val chart = BoxAndWhiskerChart(dataset,
        title="Experimental Data",
        legend=false)
      chart.plot.getDomainAxis().setLabel("Experiment No.")
      chart.plot.getRangeAxis().setLabel("Value")
      chart.show()
    }
  }
```

Saving charts to a file

If you installed scala-chart in the way advised in this section, then you will have a couple of more options for exporting your charts to file; the, **Portable Document Format (PDF)** and **Scalable Vector Graphics (SVG)** formats are supported. They have an advantage over bitmap formats such as JPEG or PNG in that pictures exported using these formats can be scaled without losing picture quality.

This is because the picture is stored as instructions on how to draw the picture in question (such as geometrical shape coordinates) rather than individual pixels. Consider our previous program that displayed a box-and-whisker plot. You can add any of the following lines to export to any of the file formats scala-chart supports after creating the `chart` object:

```
chart.saveAsPNG("test.png")
chart.saveAsJPEG("test.jpg")
chart.saveAsPDF("test.pdf")
chart.saveAsSVG("test.svg")
```

Plotting with Wisp

We now turn our attention to Wisp, which is a powerful plotting library that you can use from the Scala shell. You can, of course, also use it from your program. But the interface it provides is so minimal that using it from the console is very convenient. It will visualize plots using your default browser. It is very simple to use and is probably the fastest way to quickly visualize your data currently available in Scala. The Wisp website is given here:

```
https://github.com/quantifind/wisp
```

To enable the use of Wisp in your project, add the following line to your `build.sbt` file:

```
libraryDependencies += "com.quantifind" %% "wisp" % "0.0.4"
```

After doing that, run the following command from the shell while in the `project` directory:

sbt console

This will put you in the Scala console with the Wisp libraries loaded and ready to go. Note that, since Wisp is a large library with a lot of dependencies, it may take a while to pull them all in. Now, we can simply type in instructions and have Wisp plot them for us:

```
scala> import com.quantifind.charts.Highcharts._
import com.quantifind.charts.Highcharts._
```

First of all, we import `Highcharts`. It follows the Highcharts JavaScript plotting API and allows you to plot data using very simple commands:

```
scala> import scala.util.Random
import scala.util.Random


scala> import scala.math._
import scala.math._
```

We then import the Scala utility methods. Now we will need to generate data for use in our plot:

```
scala> val x = for (i <- 0 until 20) yield { -Pi + 2.0 * Pi * (i / 20.0) }
x: scala.collection.immutable.IndexedSeq[Double] =
Vector(-3.141592653589793, -2.827433388230814, -2.5132741228718345,
-2.199114857512855, -1.8849555921538759, -1.5707963267948966,
```

```
-1.2566370614359172, -0.9424777960769379, -0.6283185307179586,
-0.3141592653589793, 0.0, 0.31415926535897976, 0.6283185307179586,
0.9424777960769379, 1.2566370614359172, 1.5707963267948966,
1.8849555921538759, 2.199114857512855, 2.5132741228718345,
2.827433388230814)
```

```
scala> val sin_y = x.map(sin(_))
```

```
sin_y: scala.collection.immutable.IndexedSeq[Double] = Vector(-
1.2246467991473532E-16, -0.3090169943749475, -0.5877852522924732,
-0.8090169943749475, -0.9510565162951536, -1.0, -0.9510565162951535,
-0.8090169943749475, -0.5877852522924731, -0.3090169943749474,
0.0, 0.30901699437494784, 0.5877852522924731, 0.8090169943749475,
0.9510565162951535, 1.0, 0.9510565162951536, 0.8090169943749475,
0.5877852522924732, 0.3090169943749475)
```

```
scala> val cos_y = x.map(cos(_))
```

```
cos_y: scala.collection.immutable.IndexedSeq[Double] = Vector(-1.0,
-0.9510565162951535, -0.8090169943749473, -0.587785252292473,
-0.30901699437494734, 6.123233995736766E-17, 0.30901699437494745,
0.5877852522924731, 0.8090169943749475, 0.9510565162951535,
1.0, 0.9510565162951534, 0.8090169943749475, 0.5877852522924731,
0.30901699437494745, 6.123233995736766E-17, -0.30901699437494734,
-0.587785252292473, -0.8090169943749473, -0.9510565162951535)
```

We will use twenty points in our plot. For each point, the x coordinate corresponds to the argument value and the y coordinate corresponds to either *sin(x)* or *cos(x)*:

```
scala> scatter(x zip sin_y)
...
scala> hold
scala> scatter(x zip cos_y)
...
```

Then we will use `sine` function values to generate scatter plot. The `scatter` method will generate a simple scatter plot as its name implies. The argument to the scatter plot can be either a sequence of points where each point is a sequence of x and y coordinates or two sequences where the x coordinate values are in the first sequence and the y coordinate values are in the second sequence.

We have chosen the first approach here. Note the use of the hold method there. Using it means use of it makes it so that the invocation of the scatter method following it will not create a new plot but will do a scatter plot on top of the previous one. This is precisely what we want in this case. We want to have both sets of points displayed in the same plot. If later you want to plot on a new figure without restarting Wisp, you can simply do unhold and it will start drawing each plot on a separate figure again:

```scala
scala> xAxis("x")
...
scala> yAxis("y")
...
scala> title("Trigonometry")
...
scala> legend(List("sin(x)", "cos(x)"))
```

Finally, we set the values for the axis label, plot title, and legend. The legend method takes a list of values where each value will describe points in consecutive scatter plots. This means that the points created by the first scatter call will be labeled sin(x), while the points created by the second scatter call will be labeled cos(x):

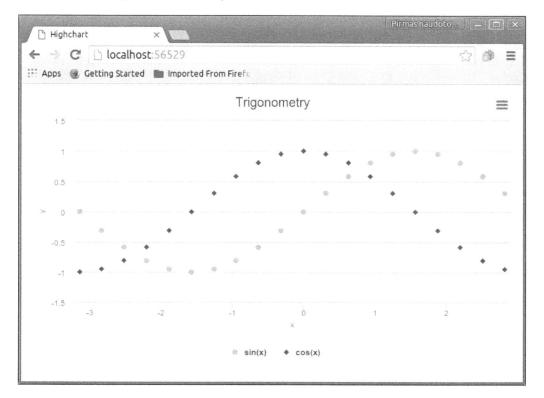

As you can see, the plot was opened via the browser. It will run the default browser automatically, but you can actually connect to the plotting server by specifying the host as localhost and the port number can be found in the console output, which will look similar to the one given here:

```
serving resources from: file:/home/vytas/scalaplotting/
index-1453408053309.html

2016-01-21 22:27:33.539:INFO:oejs.Server:jetty-8.1.13.v20130916

2016-01-21 22:27:33.588:INFO:oejs.AbstractConnector:Started
SocketConnector@0.0.0.0:56529

Server started: http://thinkpad:56529/index-1453408053309.html

Output written to http://thinkpad:56529 (CMD + Click link in Mac OSX).
```

You can even connect to this server remotely! However, I am not completely sure when you would want to.

Creating a line plot

The plot in the following figure was created using the same commands as the previous plot, except that the scatter method was replaced with the line method. The arguments for the two methods are exactly the same.

Furthermore, we used Wisp's option to download the plot as an image file. Just click on the **Options** icon (three short horizontal bars by each plot) in the browser window. It allows you to export your plots as PNG, JPEG, PDF, and SVG files:

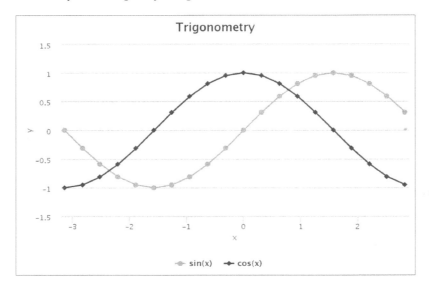

Creating a histogram

Typing the commands given here into the Scala shell will produce the histogram given in the figure. The histogram method takes two arguments, the first of which is a sequence of numerical values and the second one is the number of bins. Functionally, the code does the same thing as the code for the other two plotting systems we looked at. It is, however, arguably much simpler:

```scala
scala> val x = for (i <- 0 until 1000) yield { Random.nextGaussian() }

x: scala.collection.immutable.IndexedSeq[Double] =
Vector(0.1647482246303734, -0.5837075021516877, -2.0526504048874146,
-2.976964591908242,

...

scala> histogram(x, 11)

Output written to http://thinkpad:44390 (CMD + Click link in Mac OSX).

...

scala> title("Histogram")

...

scala> xAxis("Value")

...

scala> yAxis("Frequency")

...

scala> legend(List("Data"))

...
```

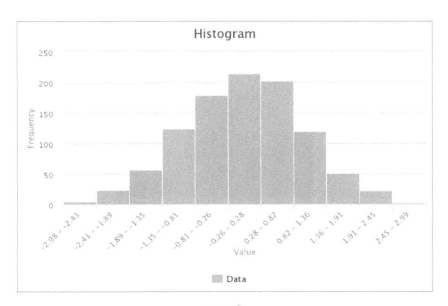

Creating a bar chart

The following console commands will produce the histogram given in the figure. It is equivalent to the histograms we produced before with one exception. There does not seem, to the best of my knowledge, to be an easy way to label the values on the *x* axis like we did previously. Therefore, instead of country names, we have the values 0 and 1. The commands themselves are really simple and should not need explanation:

```scala
scala> column(List(6, 5))
...
scala> hold

scala> column(List(7, 8))
...
scala> column(List(8, 7))
...
scala> column(List(5, 6))
...
scala> title("GDP Growth")
...
scala> xAxis("Country")
...
scala> yAxis("GDP Growth (%)")
...
scala> legend(List("Q1", "Q2", "Q3", "Q4"))
...
```

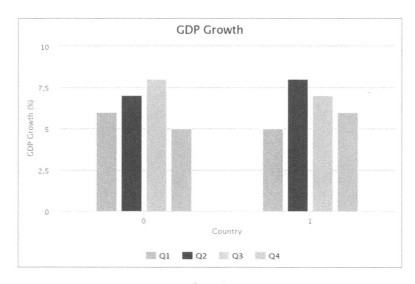

Creating a box-and-whisker chart

In the version of Wisp that is installed by following the instructions in this section, there does not seem to be a way to do a box-and-whisker type of plot. It is also not easy to produce using the functionality of existing plotting types. Therefore, we won't include one here. Hopefully, it will be introduced in the future.

Creating a linear regression plot

Wisp lets you easily create a linear regression plot, which data to a simple linear model. For a linear regression plot, both the points and the line are plotted. Actual regression is calculated by Wisp, so you barely need to do anything. See the following example:

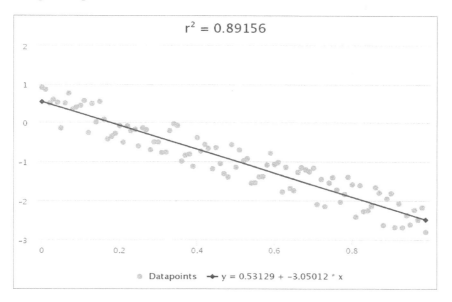

```
scala> import scala.util.Random
import scala.util.Random
scala> import com.quantifind.charts.Highcharts._
...
scala> val x = for (i <- 0 until 100) yield { i / 100.0 }
...
scala> val xs = for (i <- 0 until 100) yield { i / 100.0 }
...
scala> val ys = for (x <- xs) yield { -3.0 * x + 0.5 }
...
```

Above we have created our data by adding uniformly distributed noise to a line of the form *y = -3.0 x – 0.5* in the interval 0 to 1. The noise will range from -0.5 to 0.5 in value:

```
scala> val ysNoise = for (y <- ys) yield { y + (Random.nextDouble() -
0.5) }
...

scala> regression(xs, ysNoise)
...
```

As can be seen in the figure, the predicted model corresponds quite closely to our line. All in all, this is a convenient way for quickly performing a linear regression and visualizing the results. All you have to do is import the Wisp libraries and carry out a simple call to the `regression` method. How can it possibly get any easier than that?

Interacting with the server

It is possible to interact with the Wisp plotting server if such a need arises. This allows you to undo and redo changes, delete plots, and so on. A table with commands that pertain to the server (and an explanation of what they do) is given in the following table:

Command	Description
startServer()	This will attempt to start the plotting server.
stopServer()	This will stop the plotting server if it is running.
undo()	This will undo the last command. For example, if you issued a new plotting command, but forgot hold (or unhold), you can now undo it and fix your mistake.
redo()	This will repeat an undone command. Use it if you used undo when you did not intend to.
delete()	This deletes the last plot the user drew.
deleteAll()	This deletes all plots.

Summary

In this chapter, we looked at various possibilities for performing scientific plotting in Scala. Scientific plotting is an important part of many areas of scientific research. It allows for the easy visualization of results and for exploratory data analysis. People can more readily discern possible trends or patterns in data when it is visualized.

Currently, there aren't that many professional-quality plotting options for Scala. We looked at three possible candidates. The first of these is JFreeChart, which is a powerful plotting library written in Java. We saw how to use JFreeChart in your project and how to implement basic plot types in it. We then looked at scala-chart, which is a Scala wrapper for JFreeChart. It provides much the same functionality but more idiomatic Scala can be used to interact with it.

Then we looked at Wisp, which is a very convenient option albeit one that is not very feature-rich or powerful at the moment. It uses your web browser to display plots in an interactive manner. After reading this chapter, you should have enough information to start plotting your data using Scala.

9
Visualizing Multi-Dimensional Data in Scala

In this chapter, we will build on what you learned in the previous chapter and teach you how to use the advanced features of JFreeChart to visualize multi-dimensional data. Multi-dimensional or multi-variant data is data where separate objects, events, and so on, are described using several numerical attributes. If the number of attributes is lower than four, then visualizing this data is relatively simple.

One can use a scatter plot or its 3D equivalent. Then, one can look at the plotted data to visually ascertain its structure. If the dataset describes objects belonging to several distinct classes, for example, the relationship between the classes can be visually determined by a human analyst. However, if the dimensionality of the data is larger, there is no straightforward way of doing this. Humans are not good at thinking about points in spaces of hundreds, tens, or even five dimensions. Therefore, the data is usually processed in some way that allows it to be displayed on a (usually two-dimensional) drawing.

We will look into several such methods in this chapter. These techniques are very important to scientists. That is because one is very likely to encounter datasets such as these when analyzing almost every phenomenon in sociology, psychology, chemistry, or physics. Therefore, a way to actually look at the data with one's own eyes would be very nice. In this chapter, we will cover the following topics:

- Obtaining data to visualize
- Andrews curve
- Parallel coordinates
- Scatter plot matrix
- Sammon projection

Obtaining data to visualize

First of all, we will need multi-dimensional data to visualize. It can be thought of as a collection of rows, each with an equal number of columns (or attributes). Sometimes these rows are called records, and they usually represent the properties of some real-world or other object. For example, rows can represent a person with columns for age, height, and so on. The position of a value in the record therefore has a meaning.

Each column represents an attribute. We have already considered this type of data multiple times through out the course of this book. An example of such a dataset is the data about Iris flowers that is very commonly used as a sort of data analysis "Hello, World!" This dataset has already been explored in this book. You can get it from the website given here:

```
https://archive.ics.uci.edu/ml/datasets/Iris
```

Just save it to your project directory for it to be readily available for use in the programs we will write in this chapter. This dataset is attractive since its dimensionality is neither very small nor very large — each flower is described by five attributes. The first four of are numerical and the last one is the species of the flower.

Here we provide a Scala program that reads this dataset into a Scala Map. The key in this map is the name of the attribute (a string) and the value associated with that key is a `MutableList` containing values in that column. All values will be read as strings. It will be up to us to convert them to `Double` when needed.

A similar program has already been considered when we were talking about data storage and retrieval in Scala. As such, we will not be discussing the code at any depth. The only important thing to note is that we moved the code for reading the data into a separate method. This method accepts a `String` and returns a `Map` with data. The argument is the name of the file to be read. This little snippet will be the basis for our visualization programs that follow:

```scala
import scala.collection.mutable.{MutableList, Map}
import java.io.{FileReader, BufferedReader}

object CSVReader {
  def readCSVFile(filename: String):
    Map[String, MutableList[String]] = {
    val file = new FileReader(filename)
    val reader = new BufferedReader(file)
    val csvdata: Map[String, MutableList[String]] = Map()
    try {
      val alldata = new MutableList[Array[String]]
      var line:String = null
```

```scala
      while ({line = reader.readLine(); line} != null) {
        if (line.length != 0) {
          val delimiter: String = ","
          var splitline: Array[String] =
            line.split(delimiter).map(_.trim)
          alldata += splitline
        }
      }
      val labels = MutableList("sepal length",
                               "sepal width",
                               "petal length",
                               "petal width",
                               "class")
      val labeled = labels.zipWithIndex.map {
        case (label, index) =>
          label -> alldata.map(x => x(index))
      }
      for (pair <- labelled) {
        csvdata += pair
      }
    } finally {
      reader.close()
    }
    csvdata
  }

  def main(args: Array[String]) {
    println(readCSVFile("iris.csv"))
  }
}
```

Running the preceding program will print out the contents of the file after they have been parsed and stored in a Scala Map.

Andrews curve

Let's start with something easy. We will see how to use Andrews curve to visualize our Iris data. Andrews curve is a very simple visualization method yet it is sometimes an effective way to spot clusters in multi-dimensional data.

The way it works is really simple. Each row is plotted as a separate curve. Suppose we have a row $x = \{x_1, x_2, x_3, \ldots\}$, where x_i is the value of the ith attribute for that row. Then, the curve corresponding to this row is given here:

$$f_x(t) = \frac{x_1}{\sqrt{2}} + x_2 \sin(t) + x_3 \cos(t) + x_4 \sin(2t) + x_5 \cos(2t) + \cdots, \text{ where } -\prod <\neq< \prod.$$

Therefore, each row defines a finite Fourier series. This curve is then plotted. We will have as many curves as there are rows in our file. So in our case there will be 150 curves.

The curves that form clusters in the data will then form groups in the plot as well. This plot can sometimes be useful in exploratory data analysis. It may allow one to identify clusters in the data. It is especially useful because it works well with large numbers of attributes. The following is our implementation of the Andrews curve:

```scala
import org.jfree.chart._
import org.jfree.data.xy._
import scala.math._
import scala.collection.mutable.{MutableList, Map}
import java.io.{FileReader, BufferedReader}

object AndrewsCurve {
  def readCSVFile(filename: String):
    Map[String, MutableList[String]] = {
    ...
  }
```

The `readCSVFile` method is simply our implementation of a CSV file reader. We discussed it previously in this chapter. For the purpose of not repeating the code multiple times, we omitted the implementation of this method. Instead, it is replaced by ellipses. Refer to the previous section for implementation details. The main point is that the method takes a name of a file and returns `Map` with attribute names mapped to lists with values for that attribute in the file. Basically, it reads a CSV file column-wise:

```scala
def andrewsCurve(row: Array[Double]) = (t: Double) => {
  var result: Double = 0.0
  for ((attr, i) <- row.zipWithIndex) {
    if (i == 0) {
      result = result + row(i) / sqrt(2.0)
    } else if (i % 2 != 0) {
      result = result + row(i) * sin(((i + 1) / 2) * t)
    } else {
      result = result + row(i) * cos(((i + 1) / 2) * t)
    }
  }
  result
}
```

The preceding method will return a function that calculates the Andrews curve. This function, when given a value between -*pi* and *pi*, will return the Andrews curve value for that argument. The function itself is calculated using the formula for the Andrews curve we have given before. To produce the function for the curve, this method takes an array of doubles where each value is the value of the corresponding attribute:

```
def main(args: Array[String]) {
  val data = readCSVFile("iris.csv")
  val x: Array[Double] = Array.tabulate(100) {
    (i: Int) => -Pi + 2.0 * Pi * (i / 100.0)
  }
  val dataset = new DefaultXYDataset
  for (i <- 0 until data("sepal length").size) {
```

Here, we iterate over every row in the Iris data file. We want to collect the values of attributes and construct a separate Andrews curve for each row. After calculating the values of the Andrews curve, we add the corresponding series to our dataset:

```
    val x1 = data("sepal length")(i).toDouble
    val x2 = data("sepal width")(i).toDouble
    val x3 = data("petal length")(i).toDouble
    val x4 = data("petal width")(i).toDouble
    val cls = data("class")(i)
    val curve = x.map(andrewsCurve(Array(x1, x2, x3, x4)))
    dataset.addSeries(cls + i, Array(x, curve))
  }
  val frame = new ChartFrame("Andrews Curve",
    ChartFactory.createXYLineChart("Andrews Curve",
      "x", "y", dataset,
      org.jfree.chart.plot.PlotOrientation.VERTICAL,
      false, false, false))
  frame.pack()
  frame.setVisible(true)
  }
}
```

Finally, the results are plotted using **XYLineChart**, which is provided by JFreeChart. This was discussed in the previous section. We have chosen to display the plot in a separate window, but you may also want to save it to a file if you so prefer.

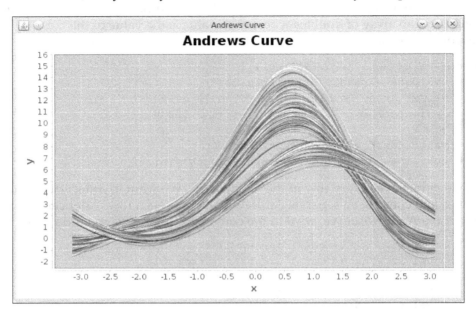

Parallel coordinates

Parallel coordinates is a common way to visualize multi-dimensional data. It is similar in principle to Andrews curve. The idea behind parallel coordinates is very simple. Each attribute is represented as a vertical line. These vertical lines are uniformly spaced. A data point is then constructed by connecting the values on the vertical lines that correspond to values of that attribute by line segments. Again, an example is helpful to illustrate how it works:

```scala
import org.jfree.chart._
import org.jfree.data.xy._
import scala.math._
import scala.collection.mutable.{MutableList, Map}
import java.io.{FileReader, BufferedReader}

object ParallelCoordinates {
  def readCSVFile(filename: String): Map[String,
  MutableList[String]] = {
    ...
  }
```

```
def main(args: Array[String]) {
  val data = readCSVFile("iris.csv")
  val dataset = new DefaultXYDataset
  for (i <- 0 until data("sepal length").size) {
    val x = Array(0.0, 1.0, 2.0, 3.0)
    val y1 = data("sepal length")(i).toDouble
    val y2 = data("sepal width")(i).toDouble
    val y3 = data("petal length")(i).toDouble
    val y4 = data("petal width")(i).toDouble
    val y = Array(y1, y2, y3, y4)
    val cls = data("class")(i)
    dataset.addSeries(cls + i, Array(x, y))
```

What is visualized here is a separate curve consisting of straight-line segments for each row in the dataset. We construct that curve by uniformly spacing values of x at (0, 1, 2, and 3) and then simply using the values of the attributes for the y values. This results in a very simple visualization method:

```
  }
  val frame = new ChartFrame("Parallel Coordinates",
    ChartFactory.createXYLineChart("Parallel Coordinates", "x",
    "y",
    dataset, org.jfree.chart.plot.PlotOrientation.VERTICAL,
    false, false, false))
  frame.pack()
  frame.setVisible(true)
  }
}
```

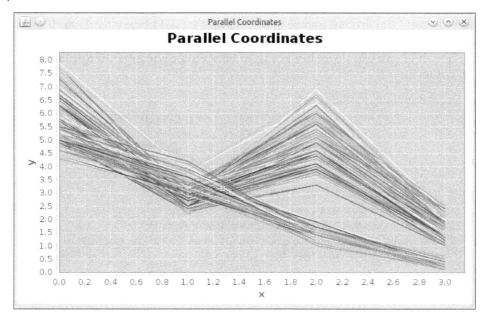

Scatter plot matrix

Scatter plot matrix is a set of scatter plots. These are constructed by considering each possible pair of attributes and plotting points using just those two attributes as a scatter plot. This will result in n times n scatter plots if n is the number of attributes. It is most convenient to arrange these plots into a rectangular matrix (hence the name).

We looked into this kind of plot earlier when we were discussing the Breeze library and its plotting framework. However, it is informative to see how this could be done in pure JFreeChart. It will also make use of most of the JFreeChart concepts that we have discussed so far:

```
import scala.collection.mutable.{MutableList, Map}
import scala.math._
import org.jfree.chart._
import org.jfree.data.xy._
import org.jfree.data.statistics._
import java.io.{FileReader, BufferedReader}
import java.awt.GridLayout
import javax.swing.JFrame
import javax.swing.Jpanel
```

Note that we will need to import some Swing stuff as well here. The reason for this is that we will have to manipulate Swing layouts directly. This is because JFreeChart does not allow subplots in the way that we require them.

For those of you who are not aware of it, Swing is a GUI library for Java. It used to be the default GUI solution for Java. It is currently in the process of being replaced by JavaFX; however, we are probably going to be seeing Swing-based applications for years to come:

```
object ScatterPlotMatrix {
  def readCSVFile(filename: String): Map[String, MutableList[String]]
= {
    ...
  }

  def main(args: Array[String]) {
    val data = readCSVFile("iris.csv")
    val frame = new JFrame("Scatter Plot Matrix")
    frame.setDefaultCloseOperation(JFrame.EXIT_ON_CLOSE)
    frame.setLayout(new GridLayout(4, 4))
```

Here, we create and set up a Swing frame on which we will display our plots. A Frame is a representation of the program window. We set it to close when the user clicks the **Close** button in the (usually) top-right corner of the window.

We also set the frame to use the grid layout. This means that panels added to the window will be arranged in a rectangular array. While the grid layout is somewhat limiting for most GUI applications, it is exactly what we need for our plot matrix:

```
val attributes = List("sepal length", "sepal width",
  "petal length", "petal width")
val classes = List("Iris-setosa", "Iris-versicolor", "Iris-
  virginica")
for ((a1, i) <- attributes.zipWithIndex) {
  for ((a2, j) <- attributes.zipWithIndex) {
```

We iterate over every possible pair of attribute names. There are four attributes in the Iris dataset we are using. This means there will be sixteen plots. However, it does not make sense to create a scatter plot when the attributes are the same. If a1 is the same as a2 in the preceding code, we will create a histogram of a1 instead. This is a good use of the space in the diagonal of our chart:

```
if (a1 == a2) {
  val dataset = new HistogramDataset();
  dataset.setType(HistogramType.RELATIVE_FREQUENCY);
  val xs = (for (x <- data(a1)) yield { x.tcDouble
  }).toArray
  dataset.addSeries(a1, xs, 11);
  val chart = ChartFactory.createHistogram(null, a1,
  "frequency",
    dataset,
    org.jfree.chart.plot.PlotOrientation.VERTICAL,
    false, false, false)
  frame.add(new ChartPanel(chart, 200, 200, 200, 200,
  200, 200,
    false, true, true, true, true, true))
```

The preceding code for calculating and drawing a histogram is basically the same as we used when discussing plotting in the previous chapter. In this case, we add the chart we created to the frame. The add method will add the plots we create to the frame, filling in the cells of the grid layout from left to right and top to bottom:

```
} else {
  val dataset = new DefaultXYDataset
  for (cls <- classes) {
    val xs = (for ((x, index) <- data(a1).zipWithIndex
```

```
            if data("class")(index) == cls)
        yield { x.toDouble }).toArray
        val ys = (for ((y, index) <- data(a2).zipWithIndex
          if data("class")(index) == cls)
        yield { y.toDouble }).toArray
        dataset.addSeries(cls, Array(xs, ys))
      }
```

We then add data series to the dataset we are going to display as a scatter plot. What we want here is to display different classes using different colors and different marker symbols.

To this end, we iterate over class names and create a different series for each of the classes. We do this by checking if the class attribute of a row has the value of the class we currently want. This is done using the **for** expression combined with **if** in the preceding code. Make sure you understand the code. This is probably the only part of the program that is not simple:

```
        val chart = ChartFactory.createScatterPlot(null,
          a1, a2, dataset,
          org.jfree.chart.plot.PlotOrientation.VERTICAL,
          false, false, false)
        frame.add(new ChartPanel(chart, 200, 200, 200,
              200, 200, 200,
          false, true, true, true, true, true))
      }
    }
  }
```

When the attributes are different, we create a scatter plot instead. It is then added to the frame in the same way we did with the histograms:

```
    frame.pack()
    frame.setVisible(true)
  }
}
```

The result of all this labor can be seen in the following figure. As you can see, there are several things that are not completely optimal with our plot. First of all, there are no reasons to display *x* and *y* axis names by every plot. This wastes screen space. The names could be displayed only at the, say, left and bottom of the plot.

Second, there is no way to display the legend conveniently when nonstandard layouts are used. If we chose to include a legend, it would be included by every subplot, thus wasting even more screen space. It is possible to address all of these points by wrestling with JFreeChart and Swing directly. However, we will leave this as an exercise for the reader.

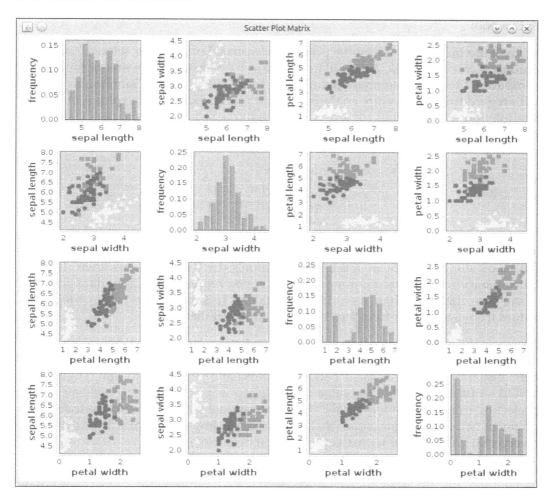

Sammon mapping

Sammon mapping is a way of projecting multi-dimensional data to a lower dimensional space. The idea behind Sammon mapping is to create a projection in which distances between points are kept the same as in the higher-dimensional space. This is probably going to be the most complicated program we have explored in this book.

We will use information from the previous chapters. For example, we will use the optimization routines we explored in the chapter dedicated to the Breeze numerical computing library. Sammon mapping was proposed by John W. Sammon in 1968 with regard to data structure analysis. It is particularly suited for exploratory data analysis, since it maintains (or aims to maintain) the structure of the data after projecting it to a lower dimensional space. To understand how Sammon mapping of a dataset is calculated, see the formula here:

$$E = \frac{1}{\sum\limits_{i<j} d_{ij}^*} \sum_{i<j} \frac{\left(d_{ij}^* - d_{ij}\right)^2}{d_{ij}^*}$$

Let's look at it term by term. E is called Sammon's stress or Sammon's error. This is the value we will want to minimize. Indices i and j represent different data points. In our case, there are 150 rows in the Iris data file. This means that i and j will take values from 0 to 149 (or from 1 to 150, if you prefer it that way).

Distance d^*ij is the distance between point i and point j in the original dataset. The distance is calculated using the Euclidean distance formula. We will not repeat it here. Distance dij is the distance between points i and j in the projection. The idea is to find a projection so that the value of E is as low as possible. In our case, we will be projecting from four-dimensional to two-dimensional space. So, we want to find 150 points in two-dimensional space that would give as low a value of E as possible. This means that we are faced with an optimization problem.

In the original method, simple gradient descent is used. We will be a bit cleverer and employ the optimization routines provided by the Breeze numerical computing library. We discussed optimization briefly in the chapter dedicated to Breeze. Let's see how to make it suit our needs here.

Since we will be using Breeze, you need the following in your `build.sbt`:

```
libraryDependencies  ++= Seq(
  "org.scalanlp" %% "breeze" % "0.10",
  "org.scalanlp" %% "breeze-natives" % "0.10"
)

resolvers ++= Seq(
  "Sonatype Releases" at "https://oss.sonatype.org/content/
repositories/releases/"
)

scalaVersion := "2.11.1"
```

With that out of the way, we can now look at the program that does the projection. The idea is simple: we minimize the Sammon error to obtain a two-dimensional projection of our four-dimensional data. We then simply plot the resulting two-dimensional points and get a nice overview of the structure of our data:

```
import org.jfree.chart._
import org.jfree.data.xy._
import java.io.{FileReader, BufferedReader}
import breeze.linalg._
import breeze.optimize._
import scala.collection.mutable.{MutableList, Map}
import scala.math._

object ScatterPlotMatrix {
  def readCSVFile(filename: String): Map[String,
  MutableList[String]] = {
    ...
  }

  def distance(x1: DenseVector[Double],
               x2: DenseVector[Double]): Double = {
    sqrt(sum((x1 - x2) :^ 2.0))
  }
}
```

The preceding code calculates the Euclidean distance between two points. The dimension of those two points does not matter with this implementation as long as it is the same for the two points.

We calculate an element-wise difference between the vectors, square the elements of the result, sum it, and return the square root of that. This will work with any two dense vectors of the `Double` data type as long as they have the same number of elements:

```
def d2(xs: DenseVector[Double], i: Int, j: Int, n: Int):
  Double = {
  distance(DenseVector(xs(i), xs(n + i)),
    DenseVector(xs(j), xs(n + j)))
}
```

The preceding code is used to calculate the distance between two vectors in the projection. It is essentially two vectors of equal length concatenated together. Each vector has the same number of elements as there are rows in the data. The first half represents the *x* coordinate and the second half represents the *y* coordinate.

In our case, the projection is a 300-element vector of type `Double`. The distance calculation is based on this representation and uses the Euclidean distance function we defined earlier:

```
def d4(xs: DenseVector[Double], i: Int, j: Int, n: Int):
Double = {
    distance(DenseVector(xs(i), xs(n + i), xs(n * 2 + i),
    xs(n * 3 + i)),
      DenseVector(xs(j), xs(n + j), xs(n * 2 + j), xs(n * 3 + j)))
}
```

The preceding code is used to calculate the distance between vectors in the original dataset. The vectors will be four-dimensional because each data entry has four attributes (not counting the class attribute). The idea behind the method is to make sure that the distances between any two points in the projection are the same as the distances between corresponding points (four-dimensional) in the original data.

We will use the preceding two functions to numerically estimate how similar those distances are. The simplest way is to use the squared difference between two distances. If we sum it up over all two row combinations this will give the amount by which the distances differ (or the Sammon error):

```
def createF(xsData: DenseVector[Double]):
DenseVector[Double] => Double = {
  val n = xsData.size / 4
  val c = sum(for (i <- 0 until n; j <- 0 until n if i < j)
  yield {
    d4(xsData, i, j, n)
  })
  xs: DenseVector[Double] => {
```

```
      val sequence = for (i <- 0 until n; j <- 0 until n if i < j)
      yield {
        val d2ij = d2(xs, i, j, n)
        val d4ij = d4(xsData, i, j, n)
        if (d4ij != 0.0) {
          (d4ij - d2ij) * (d4ij - d2ij) / d4ij
        } else {
          1000.0
        }
      }
      (1.0 / c) * sum(sequence)
    }
  }
```

The preceding code will return a function for us to minimize. It takes, as an argument, DenseVector, which contains the original dataset. This dataset has to be prepared in a certain way, by taking all the columns containing attribute values and concatenating them together. So if you have the attributes "Sepal Length", "Sepal Width", "Petal Length," and "Petal Width," you need to construct a vector that contains the values of each attribute for each row (150 elements for each vector) and simply string them together using the ++ operator. The resulting 600-element vector is then passed to this method.

The method then returns a function that takes DenseVector of type Double and returns Double. The argument to this new function is the projection (a 300-element vector) and the return value is the Sammon error. The error is calculated as was explained in the equation at the start of this section.

For each unique pair of points in the projection, we calculate the squared difference of the distance between those two points and the distance between corresponding points in the original data. This value is then scaled by the inverse of the sum of distances between all the combinations of points in the original data and that is the result of this function.

You may note a curious thing about how this function is implemented. There is an if statement that checks if the value between two points in the original dataset is zero and returns 1000.0 if it is. This is because the Iris data contains three cases, where the rows are completely identical. This is a problem because the distance there will be zero. And this will cause our error calculation to return Infinity. That's because there is a division operation that divides by the distance.

To avoid this, we use an arbitrarily large value for those cases. This may not be an elegant or correct solution, but in practice it works rather well in this case. Other than this, the calculations are straightforward. Now, it is a simple matter of gluing it all together:

```
def main(args: Array[String]) {
  val data = readCSVFile("iris.csv")
  val xs1 = (for (x <- data("sepal length"))
    yield { x.toDouble }).toArray
  val xs2 = (for (x <- data("sepal width"))
    yield { x.toDouble }).toArray
  val xs3 = (for (x <- data("petal length"))
    yield { x.toDouble }).toArray
  val xs4 = (for (x <- data("petal width"))
    yield { x.toDouble }).toArray
```

Here, we read the file in using the good-old CSV reading routine. We then extract the columns and convert `String` types to `Double` types. So now, we have an array of `Double` for each of the attributes:

```
val n = xs1.size
val xsData: DenseVector[Double] =
  new DenseVector((xs1 ++ xs2 ++ xs3 ++ xs4).toArray)
```

The final step in processing the data is to concatenate the four vectors together and create a Breeze `DenseArray` out of it:

```
val f = createF(xsData)
val df = new ApproximateGradientFunction(f)
val lbfgs = new LBFGS[DenseVector[Double]](maxIter=100, m=3)
val optimum = lbfgs.minimize(df, DenseVector.zeros(n * 2))
```

The preceding code is the heart of the program. We create a new Sammon's error function using the Iris data. Now, to perform the optimization we need the gradient of this function. We have two paths — writing the gradient calculation ourselves or using the `ApproximateGradientFunction` provided by Breeze to approximate it for us.

We chose the former since it is much easier. However, this means that the optimization procedure will run much slower. This is because at every step of the method the gradient will have to be approximated. This means that there will have to be at least 600 extra evaluations of our Sammon error function. This is due to the way that the gradient approximation works.

Finally, we minimize the function using an implementation of the Broyden–Fletcher–Goldfarb–Shanno algorithm that is provided by Breeze. We run it for 100 iterations using a vector consisting of all zeros as a starting point. From this point, the method will use the gradient information to find a locally optimal solution. After it does its work, we will be left with the optimum found by the algorithm. All we need to do now is to plot it to see the projection:

```
val x = optimum.slice(0, 150).toArray
val y = optimum.slice(150, 300).toArray
```

Because of the way we structured our program, the first 150 elements of the solution will correspond to the x coordinate of the points to plot and the other 150 elements will correspond to the y coordinate:

```
val dataset = new DefaultXYDataset
dataset.addSeries("Iris Setosa",
  Array(optimum.slice(0, 50).toArray,
    optimum.slice(150, 200).toArray))
dataset.addSeries("Iris Versicolor",
  Array(optimum.slice(50, 100).toArray,
    optimum.slice(200, 250).toArray))
dataset.addSeries("Iris Virginica",
  Array(optimum.slice(100, 150).toArray,
    optimum.slice(250, 300).toArray))
```

Furthermore, we separate the data out by the class to which the points belong. This will let us see the structure of the data. That is how the points that belong to different classes are distributed with relation to points that belong to other classes:

```
val frame = new ChartFrame("Sammon Projection of Iris Data",
  ChartFactory.createScatterPlot("Sammon Projection of Iris
  Data", "x", "y",
  dataset, org.jfree.chart.plot.PlotOrientation.VERTICAL,
  true, true, false))
frame.pack()
frame.setVisible(true)
  }
}
```

The result of all of our hard work can be seen in the figure. It is clear from the figure that the three classes are relatively well separated. This is especially true for Iris Setosa, which does not overlap with the other classes at all. The remaining two classes show a slight overlap. This is all consistent with what is known about this dataset:

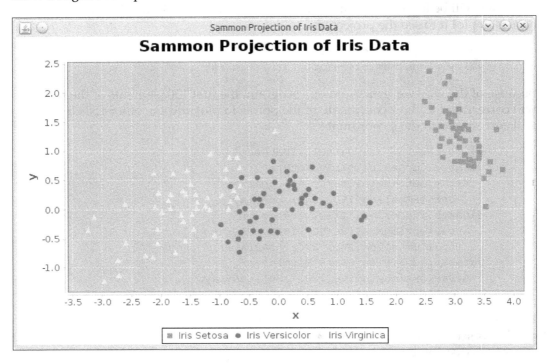

Improving the program

There is a slight improvement that we will leave as an exercise to the reader. If you run the program as it is presented here, you will note that it runs rather slowly. The reason for this is that we approximate the gradient. This is computationally costly since it involves multiple evaluations of the Sammon error function. We could do better than this. We can implement the gradient calculation ourselves. The formula to calculate the gradient is given in the equation here.

$$\frac{\partial E_s}{\partial y_{ik}} = \frac{-2}{\sum\limits_{i<j} d_{ij}} \sum\limits_{i \neq j} \frac{\left(d_{ij} - d_{ij}\right)}{d_{ij} d_{ij}} \left(y_{ik} - y_{jk}\right)$$

The notation in the equation is the same as earlier. The equation will calculate the value of the gradient at the kth coordinate of the ith vector of the approximation. Keep in mind that, since the stress function in our case is 300-dimensional, it means that to approximate the derivative you will need to evaluate the function at least 600 times (if the simplest method for approximating derivatives is used); that is, if you choose to approximate the derivative. We can implement the calculation of the partial derivative directly. To make use of the equation, you can use the following way of defining the function:

```
val f = new DiffFunction[DenseVector[Double]] {
    def calculate(x: DenseVector[Double]) = {
        ...
        (value, gradient)
    }
}
```

Here, the value is the value of the function when passed the argument x and gradient is a `DenseVector` that contains the value of the partial derivative for each coordinate. So, for our function, it will be a 300-dimensional vector. The reader is encouraged to define such a function and run the optimizer with it.

Summary

In this chapter, we looked into carrying out multi-dimensional data visualization in Scala. We used JFreeChart for plotting and Breeze for optimization. Four different techniques for visualizing multi-dimensional data were considered. The first two are very simple methods that plot each of the rows in the dataset in one way or another. This presents an overview of the data.

We then looked at how you can use JFreeChart to produce a scatter plot matrix. This is a very useful tool for quickly visualizing data. It is very useful especially because it does not lose any information in the process. If the dimensionality of your dataset is fairly low, it can be used to quickly get a feel for your data.

Finally, we looked at a more involved technique called Sammon projection. It lowers the dimensionality of your data by preserving relative distances between data points. To this end, techniques from mathematical optimization are employed. We use optimization routines provided by the Breeze numerical computing library. After reading this chapter, readers will have an idea about how to start visualizing their data in Scala.

Hopefully, by now you have an understanding of how to use Scala and its libraries for your scientific computing needs. The scientific computing tool set available from Scala is constantly expanding and being refined. After reading this book, you should be able to make good use of it for common tasks.

Index

www.ingramcontent.com/pod-product-compliance
Lightning Source LLC
Chambersburg PA
CBHW060550060326
40690CB00017B/3662